WM. K. WIDGER JR.

CULBERTSON'S
SUMMARY
of CONTRACT BRIDGE

IMPROVED
Culbertson System

By

ELY CULBERTSON

**Editor, The Bridge World Magazine; Author of
The Official Book of Contract Bridge;
Culbertson's Self-Teacher, etc., etc.**

Edited by **JOSEPHINE CULBERTSON** *and*
ALBERT H. MOREHEAD

THE JOHN C. WINSTON COMPANY
CHICAGO   PHILADELPHIA   TORONTO

HOW TO USE THIS SUMMARY

This Summary is a Quick Reference Book. It is designed to tell at a glance

1. What you need for any bid, lead or play.

2. What bid, lead or play you should make at any point in the game.

3. What you can expect your partner to hold when he bids, leads or plays.

It is entirely permissible to refer to this book during a game. The thumb indexing permits you to open immediately at the page on which is given the information you need. Being small and flexible, this Summary may conveniently be carried in your pocket or hand-bag.

As 98% of all players use the Culbertson system, the rules given in this Summary are proper for any game. They comprise all the latest features of The Culbertson System. The bidding advice given in this book is based on, and is entirely consistent with, the latest Laws of Contract Bridge.

The best of summaries can do no more than summarize. For instruction, with reasoned explanations of all bids and plays, read "The Official Culbertson System of Contract Bridge" (*The Official Book*) or "Culbertson's Self-Teacher."

A full share of the credit for this Summary must go to Josephine Culbertson and Albert H. Morehead, who edited it; to Alphonse Moyse, managing editor of The Bridge World Magazine, and to George L. Bard.

ELY CULBERTSON

HOW TO VALUE YOUR HAND

Honor-tricks are cards or card combinations which may be expected to win tricks *whatever the final contract is*—even as *defensive* tricks against opponents' bids.

CULBERTSON STANDARD TABLE OF
═ HONOR-TRICKS ═

IF YOU HAVE	COUNT
A-K (or A-K-J) in the same suit A-K-Q = 2 + honor-tricks	**2** honor-tricks
A-Q (or A-Q-J) in the same suit	**1½** honor-tricks
Ace (or A-J alone) **K-Q** (or K-Q-10) in the same suit **K-J-10** in the same suit K-x and K-x = 1 honor-trick A-J-x or K-Q-J = 1 + honor-trick	**1** honor-trick
K-x* (or K-J alone) **Q-J-x** Q-x and Q-x = ½ honor-trick K-J-x = ½ + honor-trick	**½** honor-trick Any two half honor-tricks equal 1 honor-trick.
Any singleton or void Only one singleton (or void) may be counted **Queen** in Q-x or in A-K-Q **Jack** in K-Q-J, A-J-x or K-J-x	**+** A PLUS VALUE Any two plus values are equivalent to ½ honor-trick.

When you bid a 4-card suit, or bid notrump, *count your honor-cards*. Hand solidity may offset distributional weakness. *An honor-card is any A, K, Q, J or 10.* If you have a total of *SIX* or more honor-cards in your hand, add a *plus value* to your honor-trick count.

* The symbol "x" applies to any lower card in the suit.

4

HOW HIGH TO GO IN BIDDING

The four players in the game hold a combined total of 8 to 8½ honor-tricks in every deal. This is based on the famous Culbertson Rule of Eight, given below.

Every time your partner bids, his bid guarantees a certain minimum number of honor-tricks.

Add your own honor-trick total to the number of honor-tricks partner's bids have guaranteed (page 40). Subtract the combined total from 8½. The difference is the honor-tricks your opponents hold.

As your *opponents'* honor-tricks will probably win against your contract, you can tell how high you can safely bid.

As *your* honor-tricks will probably win against your opponents' contract, you can tell when they have overbid and you can defeat their contract.

The Rule of Eight

In the average deal, 8 to 8½ out of 13 tricks will be won by honor-tricks; 4½ to 5 tricks will be won by lower cards.

When your side plays the hand, for whatever honor-tricks you hold you may expect also to win low-card tricks in the ratio of about 5 to 8.

In the combined partnership hands,

 to 4½ honor-tricks will produce about ONE-ODD in notrump (or down one) TWO-ODD in the best available trump suit.

5 to 5½ honor-tricks will produce about TWO-ODD (usually less than game) in notrump. Only two- or three-odd at a trump contract with a fair fit, but GAME in a major suit if combined partnership hands have 8 to 10 cards in their trump suit and unbalanced distribution.

 honor-tricks in the combined hands promise GAME either at notrump (three-odd) or at four-odd in a major suit, if available.

With 6½ or more honor-tricks in the combined hands you are in the Slam Zone but a successful Slam will depend upon many other factors (page 44).

5

THESE SUITS ARE BIDDABLE

A biddable suit is a suit (always of 4 cards*
or longer) that may be bid if the hand as a
whole is strong enough.

Partner should always expect that any suit bid
is at least 4 cards in length and genuinely biddable
in accordance with the following table:

HOLDING	WHEN TO BID IT
Q-x-x-x (4 cards) up to A-10-x-x **X-X-X-X-X** (5 cards) up to J-x-x-x-x	**CONDITIONAL** *Biddable Suits* May be bid by the opener *only when the hand contains two or more 4-card biddable suits, or in hands of extra honor-trick strength.* May be bid by the responder *at the level of one only.* Should not be rebid unless partner has raised TWICE.
Q-J-x-x up to A-K-x-x, etc. **Q-X-X-X-X,** J-10-x-x-x, or better	**REGULAR** *Biddable Suits* May be bid *once*, but should not be rebid unless partner has raised.
X-X-X-X-X-X (any 6 cards) **K-J-x-x-x** **Q-J-9-x-x**	**REBIDDABLE SUITS** May be bid and then rebid *once*. But a *free* rebid should not be made in a suit of *minimum* rebiddable strength—see page 39.
K-Q-J-x-x-x (6 cards) **Q-J-x-x-x-x-x** **K-x-x-x-x-x-x** (7 cards) or better	Should be bid and rebid *twice or more* even without support, if the total strength of the hand warrants it. See also pages 30 and 31 for treatment of stronger suits.

* *Sometimes, for want of a better opening bid, experts bid a 3-card minor no weaker than Q-10-x, and usually A-J-x or better; but they do so only as a choice of evils, and in so doing they consciously deceive their partners.*

WHEN TO OPEN THE BIDDING

1. Count your honor-tricks (page 4).

2. Look for a biddable suit (page 6). With two or more biddable suits, see pages 8–9.

3. Make an opening bid, vulnerable or not, first, second, third or fourth hand, as follows:

Honor Tricks	WHAT YOU SHOULD DO
2 or less	**PASS** *Exception:* A shut-out bid on a 7- or 8-card suit (pages 30–31) ♠ Q-J-8-6-5-4 ♡ A-J-6 ◇ Q-7 ♣ 4-3 *Pass*
2+	BID a 6-card *major* suit. *Bid one spade:* ♠ K-Q-8-6-5-2 ♡ 10-7 ◇ A-8-4-3 ♣ 6 Otherwise, PASS
2½	BID *any* rebiddable suit. *Bid one spade:* ♠ A-Q-8-5-4 ♡ K-9-7 ◇ K-6-4 ♣ 8-3 *Bid one diamond:* ♠ A-Q-6 ♡ 8-4-3 ◇ K-J-5-4-2 ♣ Q-5 Otherwise, PASS
3	BID any biddable suit. *Bid one diamond on:* ♠ 8-6-4 ♡ A-K-2 ◇ Q-J-8-6 ♣ K-4-3 *or* ♠ A-6 ♡ 10-9-5 ◇ K-7-6-4-3 ♣ A-Q-3 Do not forget to count your *honor-cards* (page 4) and add a plus value if you have 6 or more. Thus: *Bid one spade on:* ♠ K-Q-J-8 ♡ Q-J-7-3 ◇ A-8-5 ♣ 7-4
3½ to **4**	BID ONE NOTRUMP on a 4-3-3-3 (sometimes a 4-4-3-2) hand (page 25) BID any biddable suit *Do not pass*
About **5** or more	PREFER an opening two-notrump bid (page 27) or a forcing two-bid (page 28) if your hand justifies it. Otherwise, BID any biddable suit.

7

WHICH SUIT TO BID FIRST

With two biddable suits, at least one of which is 5 cards or longer, generally bid first *the longer suit when they are unequal in length,* and *the higher-ranking suit when they are equal in length.* However, the following table covers specific cases:

WITH TWO BIDDABLE SUITS

Divided	Your Choice Should Be
5-5 or **6-6**	Bid the higher ranking. *Bid one spade on:* ♠ Q-8-5-3-2 ♡ A-K-Q-4-3 ◇ 9-2 ♣ 9 *or* ♠ 10-8-6-4-3-2 ♡ — ◇ A-K-10-7-3-2 ♣ 8
5-4 With 4 or more honor-tricks	Bid the longer suit first. *Bid one diamond on:* ♠ A-K-Q-4 ♡ 8-3 ◇ A-K-9-6-5 ♣ 7-2
5-4 With less than 4 honor-tricks	Bid the higher ranking when the suits are *"touching"* in rank. Bid the longer suit when they are *not touching.* *Bid one spade on:* ♠ A-J-8-4 ♡ A-9-7-5-2 ◇ K-10-4 ♣ 6 *Bid one club on:* ♠ 9-5 ♡ A-K-7-3 ◇ Q-6 ♣ K-J-8-5-4
6-5 or **7-6**	Bid the longer suit first, then bid the shorter suit TWICE. *Bid one diamond on:* ♠ A-J-5-3-2 ♡ 10 ◇ K-Q-10-7-4-3 ♣ 6 *or* ♠ A-Q-8-7-4-2 ♡ — ◇ K-9-8-7-6-4-3 ♣ —
6-4 or **7-5**	Bid the longer suit TWICE, then show the shorter suit *Exception:* When you can show the shorter suit by a rebid at the level of one. With ♠ 6-5 ♡ A-J-8-3 ◇ 4 ♣ A-K-9-7-6-2 Bid one club. If partner responds one spade, bid two clubs. But if partner responds one diamond, bid one heart.

CHOICE BETWEEN 4-CARD SUITS

As a simple rule which is easy to remember: With two 4-card biddable suits, one of which is clubs, bid **one club**; lacking a club suit, first bid the **higher-ranking** suit.

But no rule is perfect for this difficult choice. Experts judge each hand separately by preparation to rebid safely over any forcing response. The following tables give specific advice which will provide safety in most cases:

YOUR SUITS	YOUR FIRST BID
4 Spades or Hearts and 4 Clubs	**ONE CLUB.** *Bid one club on:* ♠ A-K-8-4 ♡ 9-2 ◇ 8-6-3 ♣ K-Q-4-3 or ♠ 9-6 ♡ A-Q-J-5 ◇ Q-6-3 ♣ A-Q-8-2
4 Spades and 4 Hearts	**ONE SPADE.** *Bid one spade on:* ♠ K-9-6-2 ♡ K-J-10-4 ◇ A-Q-6 ♣ 8-4 or ♠ Q-J-10-8 ♡ A-K-6-5 ◇ 9-6-5 ♣ A-3
4 Hearts and 4 Diamonds	**ONE HEART.** *Bid one heart on:* ♠ 9-6 ♡ A-6-3-2 ◇ A-K-Q-8 ♣ 7-5-2 or ♠ A-K ♡ Q-J-8-6 ◇ Q-J-4-3 ♣ 10-9-5
4 Diamonds and 4 Clubs	**ONE DIAMOND.** *Bid one diamond on:* ♠ 8-6-3 ♡ K-9 ◇ A-K-7-6 ♣ A-Q-9-4 *But with minimum hands bid one club:* ♠ 8-6-3 ♡ 10-7 ◇ A-K-7-6 ♣ A-J-9-4
4 Spades and 4 Diamonds	**Usually Bid the Stronger Suit** *but with support for* **hearts,** *bid* **one spade;** *with support for* **clubs** *bid* **one diamond.** *Bid one spade on:* ♠ K-J-6-4 ♡ Q-7-3 ◇ A-K-5-2 ♣ 4-3

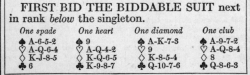

=== **With 4-4-4-1** ===

FIRST BID THE BIDDABLE SUIT next in rank *below* the singleton.

One spade	*One heart*	*One diamond*	*One club*
♠ A-6-5-2	♠ 9	♠ A-K-7-3	♠ A-9-7-2
♡ A-Q-6-4	♡ A-Q-4-2	♡ 9	♡ A-Q-8-4
◇ K-J-8-5	◇ K-Q-6-5	◇ K-8-5-4	◇ 8
♣ 6	♣ K-9-8-7	♣ Q-10-7-6	♣ Q-8-6-3

ee also
Part-Score
idding"
n page 41

GAME-FORCING BIDS

A *forcing* bid is a demand to partner not to let the bidding die until you have had *another* chance to bid.

The following bids obligate *both partners* to make sure the bidding is kept open until their side bids game (or makes a penalty double).

1. Any opening two-bid in a suit, even when there is a part-score (page 28). But an opening two-notrump bid is not forcing (page 27).

Example:				*Exception:*			
SOUTH	WEST	NORTH	EAST	SOUTH	WEST	NORTH	EAST
Pass	Pass	2 ◊ (*Forcing*)		Pass	2 N T (*Not forcing*)		

2. A jump bid (exactly one trick more than necessary) in a new suit by either partner at any time.

SOUTH	WEST	NORTH	EAST	SOUTH	WEST	NORTH	EAST
1 ♡	Pass	3 ◊ (*Forcing*)		1 ♡	Pass	1 N T	Pass
		or 2 ♠ (*Forcing*)		3 ♣ (*Forcing*)			

SOUTH	WEST	NORTH	EAST	SOUTH	WEST	NORTH	EAST
1 ♡	1 ♠	Pass	3 ♣	1 ♡	Double	Pass	2 ◊
(*Forcing for one round only*)				Pass	3 ♠ (*Forcing*)		

Only exception: When partner has not made any bid.

SOUTH	WEST	NORTH	EAST
1 ♡	1 ♠	Pass	Pass
3 ♣ *Strong but not forcing.* North may now pass unless he has about 1 honor-trick or support for one of South's suits.			

3. A bid in the opponents' suit (pages 35 and 45) by any player at any time is forcing to game.

SOUTH	WEST	NORTH	EAST	SOUTH	WEST	NORTH	EAST
1 ♡	1 ♠	2 ◊	Pass	1 ♡	Pass	1 ♠	2 ♠
2 ♠ (*Forcing*)							(*Forcing*)

Exception: When at his last previous opportunity he has doubled that suit, for takeout or penalties:				SOUTH	WEST	NORTH	EAST
				1 ♠	Double	Pass	2 ◊
				Pass	2 ♠ (*Not forcing*)		

4. A double raise (page 16) in the suit in which partner opened the bidding; or

5. A jump response of two notrump (page 16) to partner's opening bid:

But a double raise or two-notrump response is not forcing when partner has passed originally, or when, with a part-score, game has already been reached.

SOUTH	WEST	NORTH	EAST	SOUTH	WEST	NORTH	EAST
1 ♠	Pass	3 ♠ (*Forcing*)		Pass	Pass	1 ♠	Pass
		or 2 N T (*Forcing*)		3 ♠ (*NOT forcing*)			
						or 2 N T (*NOT forcing*)	

ONE-ROUND-FORCING BIDS

See also "Reverse Bidding," on page 17

When a player makes a one-round-forcing bid, his partner must keep the bidding open by responding *once* (unless there is an intervening bid or double by an opponent). But the player who makes a bid which is forcing for one round only is not *himself* obligated to rebid (unless his partner's response is, in turn, forcing).

1. Any non-jump response in a new suit to an opening suit-bid of one, unless the responder has passed originally.

Example:				Exception:			
SOUTH	WEST	NORTH	EAST	SOUTH	WEST	NORTH	EAST
1 ♡	Pass	1 ♠ (*Forcing*)		Pass	Pass	1 ♡	Pass
		or 2 ♣ (*Forcing*)		1 ♠ (*NOT forcing*)			

A suit takeout is not, however, forcing (even for one round) when because of a part-score a game contract has already been reached.

A suit *rebid* by either partner (even at the level of one) is not forcing unless it is a jump bid.

SOUTH	WEST	NORTH	EAST	SOUTH	WEST	NORTH	EAST
1 ◇	Pass	1 ♡	Pass	1 ◇	Pass	1 ♡	Pass
1 ♠ (*Not forcing*)				2 ♣ (*Not forcing*)			

2. Any conventional slam try (pages 46-47).

3. Any response of one notrump by a player whose side has a part-score of 30, 40 or 50 (see Part-Score Bidding, page 41).

OTHER FORCING BIDS

In general, when both partners have made strong, though not necessarily forcing bids, and when the combined honor-count may be assumed to be 6 or more, both partners are expected to continue bidding until game is reached.

Especially when a non-forcing, strength-showing rebid has been made by *either* partner (pages 17, 22), and the other partner has responded, the *situation* is considered forcing on both partners to reach a game.

SOUTH	WEST	NORTH	EAST	SOUTH	WEST	NORTH	EAST
1 ♡	Pass	1 ♠	Pass	1 ♡	Pass	2 ◇	Pass
2 N T	Pass	3 ♡ (*Forcing*)		2 ♠	Pass	2 N T (*Forcing*)	

See also Sign-off and Preference Bids (page 24).

WHEN TO RAISE PARTNER'S SUIT

Usually raise partner's *major* suit if you can, but *do not raise a minor* if you can take out in a suit or bid two notrump (pages 15–16).

The minimum trump strength required is:

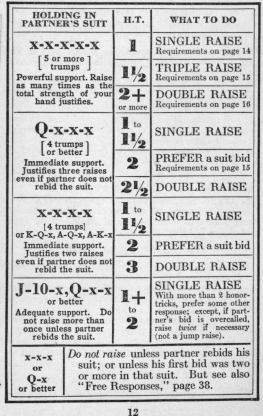

HOLDING IN PARTNER'S SUIT	H.T.	WHAT TO DO
X-X-X-X-X [5 or more trumps] Powerful support. Raise as many times as the total strength of your hand justifies.	**1**	SINGLE RAISE Requirements on page 14
	1½	TRIPLE RAISE Requirements on page 15
	2+ or more	DOUBLE RAISE Requirements on page 16
Q-x-x-x [4 trumps or better] Immediate support. Justifies three raises even if partner does not rebid the suit.	**1** to **1½**	SINGLE RAISE
	2	PREFER a suit bid Requirements on page 15
	2½	DOUBLE RAISE
X-X-X-X [4 trumps] or K-Q-x, A-Q-x, A-K-x Immediate support. Justifies two raises even if partner does not rebid the suit.	**1** to **1½**	SINGLE RAISE
	2	PREFER a suit bid
	3	DOUBLE RAISE
J-10-x, Q-x-x or better Adequate support. Do not raise more than once unless partner rebids the suit.	**1+** to **2**	SINGLE RAISE With more than 2 honor-tricks, prefer some other response; except, if partner's bid is overcalled, raise *twice* if necessary (not a jump raise).
x-x-x or **Q-x** or better	*Do not raise* unless partner rebids his suit; or unless his first bid was two or more in that suit. But see also "Free Responses," page 38.	

RESPONSES TO ONE-BIDS

When your partner makes an opening suit-bid of one, *and the next player passes,** check up on your honor-tricks, your trump support (opposite page) and your biddable suits, then respond as follows:

You will find complete requirements for all Responses on next three pages

HONOR-TRICKS	PROPER RESPONSE
0	PASS *Only exception:* Bid a 7-card *major* suit
½	USUALLY, PASS But bid ONE in a 6-card suit
1	RAISE with 4 trumps BID ONE in a 5-card suit (Bid one notrump with two suits stopped) Lacking these values, PASS
1+ to **1½**	BID ONE in *any* biddable suit BID TWO in a 6-card suit RAISE with Adequate Support BID ONE NOTRUMP
2	BID ONE in *any* biddable suit BID TWO in a 6-card suit RAISE with Adequate Support BID ONE NOTRUMP
2½ to **3**	DOUBLE RAISE with 4 trumps BID *any* biddable suit BID TWO NOTRUMP DO NOT bid only one notrump or raise only once
3½	FORCING TAKEOUT if able DOUBLE RAISE with 4 trumps BID *any* biddable suit BID TWO NOTRUMP
4 or more	FORCING TAKEOUT if able Otherwise, bid any biddable suit; or bid THREE notrump with a 4-3-3-3, but do not bid only two notrump or give a double raise

* For *Free* Responses after a double or overcall, see page 38.

13

NEGATIVE RESPONSES
Which Warn of Possible Weakness

As an opening suit-bid of one, sometimes made with only 2+ honor-tricks, may conceal extremely strong distribution or as many as 5 bare honor-tricks, the following responses may be made on quite weak hands to keep the bidding open and assure the opener a chance to show his full strength by a rebid.

THE ONE-NOTRUMP RESPONSE

A response of one notrump *denies* strength. The responding hand cannot have more than 2+ honor-tricks and often has only 1 honor-trick with stoppers (page 53) in two suits. You need:

1 to **1+** honor-trick in two suits

Otherwise **1½** to **2+** honor-tricks

Prefer a raise or suit takeout, if available, except with 4-3-3-3 distribution. With 1 honor-trick in two suits, prefer a one-over-one response even in a conditional suit (page 6).

Examples, partner's opening bid having been one spade:
1. ♠ A-6-3 ♡ Q-8-5-4 ◇ 9-8-5 ♣ 6-4-2   One notrump
2. ♠ 10-6   ♡ 9-8-5-4 ◇ A-Q-6-3 ♣ 9-8-6 One notrump
3. ♠ 9-8   ♡ 9-8-5-4 ◇ Q-8-6-3 ♣ A-K-7 One notrump

THE SINGLE RAISE

A raise of partner's suit to two sometimes shows only about 1 honor-trick, and never more than 2+. The requirements are:

With 4 Trumps } **1** honor-trick

With J-10-x, Q-x-x, etc. } **1+** honor-trick

Examples, partner having bid one heart:
1. ♠ 6   ♡ 7-5-3-2 ◇ K-J-6-4 ♣ 7-5-4-3 Two hearts
2. ♠ K-6   ♡ Q-8-5-3 ◇ 9-6-5-2 ♣ Q-7-4   Two hearts
3. ♠ 9-8-4-3 ♡ K-Q-7   ◇ 6   ♣ 10-9-7-6-3 Two hearts
4. ♠ A-9   ♡ Q-J-3   ◇ 8-6-5-2 ♣ K-6-5-3 Two hearts
Exception: With bare requirements for a raise *pass* with 4-3-3-3 distribution and all your high-card strength in one suit.
5. ♠ 8-5-3 ♡ A-7-6-4 ◇ 10-8-2   ♣ 9-4-2   Pass

14

ENCOURAGING RESPONSES

Prefer a game-forcing response if able—see page

A ONE-OVER-ONE TAKEOUT

A one-over-one takeout is *forcing for one round*, and ranges from ½ to 4 honor-tricks.

Minimum:
- ½ honor-trick, 6-card suit
- 1 honor-trick, 5-card suit
- 1 + honor-trick, 4-card suit
- (or 1 honor-trick in *two* suits)

Examples, partner having bid one club:

1.	♠ Q-J-6-5-3-2	♡ 9-6	◇ 7-4-3	♣ 5-4	One spade
2.	♠ A-6	♡ 9-7-4	◇ J-8-6-5-4	♣ 7-6-3	One diamond
3.	♠ 10-3	♡ A-J-7-2	◇ 9-6-4-3	♣ 8-6-5	One heart
4.	♠ K-6	♡ 8-7-6-2	◇ K-7-5-3	♣ 8-5-4	One diamond
5.	♠ A-K-Q-6	♡ A-8	◇ K-J-9-3	♣ 8-5-4	One spade

A TWO-OVER-ONE TAKEOUT

With a lower-ranking suit, the responder must raise the level of bidding to show his biddable suit, and needs a fairly strong hand:

1½ honor-tricks, 6-card suit
(or strong support for partner's suit)

2 honor-tricks, 5-card suit
(slightly less with a 5-card major)

2½ honor-tricks, 4-card suit

With a 7-card suit ½ to 1 honor-trick is enough. The two-over-one takeout is one-round-forcing, *but prefer a jump forcing takeout if the hand justifies it (next page).*

Examples, partner having bid one spade:

1.	♠ 8-5	♡ Q-J-2	◇ K-J-10-6-5-4	♣ 9-3	Two diamonds
2.	♠ K-6	♡ 8-6-3	◇ K-9-4-3-2	♣ A-5-4	Two diamonds
3.	♠ 8-6-4-3	♡ 9	◇ K-6-3	♣ K-Q-8-5-2	Two clubs
4.	♠ 6	♡ A-7-4-3	◇ Q-8-5-2	♣ A-Q-9-5	Two clubs

A TRIPLE RAISE

A raise of partner's suit to four is a shut-out bid (page 30). It shows:

X-X-X-X-X (5 cards or more) in trumps

1 to **1½** honor-tricks including a singleton or void (usually a 5-5-2-1 or 6-5-1-1 hand)

Examples, partner having bid one heart:

1.	♠ 6	♡ Q-8-7-5-2	◇ A-7-6-5-3	♣ 8-2	Four hearts
2.	♠ 6-5	♡ 9-7-6-5-3-2	◇ K-J-6-4-3	♣ —	Four hearts

*rcing
*ut and
*g Rebid
*rcing
*with a
*Score (see
41)

VERY STRONG RESPONSES

All of Which Are Forcing to Game

THE FORCING TAKEOUT

A jump suit takeout *of exactly one trick more than
necessary* requires

3½ honor-tricks with a solid suit or strong support for partner's suit

4 honor-tricks with a biddable suit and at least Adequate Support for partner

4½ honor-tricks with any biddable suit

Examples, partner having bid one heart:
1. ♠ 3 ♡ Q-10-5-4 ◇ A-J-5 ♣ A-K-10-8-2 Three clubs
2. ♠ A-K-J-8-6-5-2 ♡ 3 ◇ A-Q-4-3 ♣ 6 Two spades
3. ♠ A-K-7-5 ♡ K-6 ◇ A-K-4 ♣ 7-6-3-2 Two spades

THE TWO NOTRUMP TAKEOUT

A jump response of two notrump requires

3 to **3½** honor-tricks

Every unbid suit stopped

Balanced distribution and usually no biddable suit

Prefer a double raise, if available, when partner's
suit is a major. With 6 honor-cards, or when you
have passed originally, 2½ honor-tricks are enough.

Examples, partner having bid one heart:
1. ♠ A-6-3 ♡ Q-7-5 ◇ K-10-8-4 ♣ A-J-5 Two notrump
2. ♠ A-Q ♡ J-9-4 ◇ K-10-5-3 ♣ K-8-7-6 Two notrump

A DOUBLE RAISE

A jump raise of partner's suit to three requires

IN TRUMPS	MINIMUM IN HONOR-TRICKS	
X-X-X-X-X	**2+**	of which at least 1+ should be outside the trump suit
Q-x-x-x or J-10-x-x	**2½**	of which at least 1½ should be outside the trump suit.
X-X-X-X	**3**	with any distribution

Examples, partner having bid one spade:
1. ♠ A-10-9-7-6 ♡ 6-5-3-2 ◇ K-Q-8 ♣ 7 Three spades
2. ♠ K-8-5-4 ♡ A-7-6 ◇ J-8-5-2 ♣ A-7 Three spades
3. ♠ 9-6-5-3 ♡ 8-6-4 ◇ A-Q-7 ♣ A-Q-10 Three spades

Prefer two notrump or a suit takeout, if available,
when partner's suit is a minor.

STRENGTH-SHOWING REBIDS

See next
pages for
of all Rebi

Situation: You have opened with *one in a suit.* Partner has made a minimum suit or notrump response. With 4 or more honor-tricks, consider the following rebids:

A **FORCING REBID** is a jump of exactly one trick more than necessary in a new suit, requiring 5 honor-tricks (4 to 4½ with a 5-5 or 6-5 two-suiter) and a second biddable suit

GAME-GOI
BIDS

Prefer a forcing rebid to an immediate jump raise with 4 to 4½ honor-tricks.

You opened one diamond.   Partner responded one heart.   Rebid:
1. ♠ 6 ♡ K-J-3 ◇ A-K-7-5-2 ♣ A-K-J-7   Three clubs
2. ♠ A-K-J-7-3 ♡ 6 ◇ A-K-8-7-6-3 ♣ 9   Two spades
3. ♠ — ♡ K-J-5-3 ◇ A-J-8-5-4 ♣ A-K-6-5   Three clubs

A **JUMP SUIT REBID to THREE** of the suit you bid first shows

3½ honor-tricks with a strong 7-card suit
4   honor-tricks with a strong 6-card suit
4½-5 honor-tricks with a strong 5-card suit

With 8 sure winners you need ½ honor-trick less.

You opened one heart.   Partner responded one notrump.   Rebid:
1. ♠ 6 ♡ K-Q-J-7-6-5-2 ◇ A-6-3 ♣ A-4   Three hearts
2. ♠ A-6 ♡ A-J-10-7-6-3 ◇ 5 ♣ A-Q-7-5   Three hearts
3. ♠ 9 ♡ A-K-Q-J-4 ◇ A-K-Q ♣ 10-8-5-3   Three hearts

A **JUMP TO TWO NOTRUMP** as a rebid shows 4½ honor-tricks (rarely, 4 honor-tricks with 8 or 9 honor-cards), balanced distribution, and every suit stopped. It may conceal a rebiddable 5-card suit, or support for partner's suit.

You opened one heart.   Partner responded one spade.   Rebid:
1. ♠ J-5 ♡ K-Q-6-5-3 ◇ A-K-6 ♣ A-Q-10   Two notrump
2. ♠ A-J-3 ♡ A-J-8-4 ◇ K-Q-6-3 ♣ A-8   Two notrump

A **REVERSE BID** is a rebid of *two or more* in a suit higher in rank than the suit you first bid. It usually shows about 4 honor-tricks.

You opened one diamond.   Partner responded one notrump.   Rebid:
♠ A-Q-8-5 ♡ 3 ◇ A-K-7-6-2 ♣ K-5-4   Two spades

In general, any rebid of two notrump or three in any suit, including a raise of partner's suit to three, and whether a jump bid or not, shows a strong hand with at least 3½ honor-tricks and usually more.

REBIDS BY THE OPENER
When Partner Has Responded

Situation: You have made an opening suit-bid of one. Partner's *response* was a suit takeout. You *must* rebid (except when partner passed originally). Rebids are listed in order of preference.

PARTNER'S RESPONSE	If You Hold	YOUR REBID SHOULD BE
ONE-OVER-ONE	**3+** or less	RAISE with adequate support BID ONE in any new suit. With unbalanced distribution, show any rebiddable or new suit, even at two* REBID a 6-card suit Otherwise, BID ONE NOTRUMP
ONE-OVER-ONE	**3½**	SHOW any rebiddable or new suit* Otherwise, REBID as above
TWO-OVER-ONE	**3+** or less	RAISE partner's suit with 4 trumps SHOW a new suit* REBID a rebiddable suit
TWO-OVER-ONE	**3½**	RAISE with Q-x-x, J-10-x, or better Bid TWO NOTRUMP Bid TWO in a suit*
ANY SUIT TAKEOUT	**4** to **4½**	RAISE TWICE with 4 trumps JUMP to THREE in a 6-card major SHOW any new biddable suit BID TWO NOTRUMP
ANY SUIT TAKEOUT	**5** or more	Make a FORCING REBID (page 17), Bid THREE NOTRUMP, or RAISE partner's suit to game with strong trump support

* But do not "reverse"—page 17.

Important:
See also
"Free Rebid
on page 39

REBIDS B
OPENER

PARTNER'S RESPONSE / If You Hold		YOUR REBID SHOULD BE
ONE NOTRUMP	**3½** or less	REBID a 6-card suit SHOW a new 5-card suit BID two in a 4-card suit with unbalanced distribution* Lacking these values, PASS
	About **4**	REBID any rebiddable suit or SHOW a new biddable suit *See also Strength-Showing Rebids, page 17* Lacking these values, PASS
	4½	JUMP to THREE in a strong 6-card suit RAISE to TWO NOTRUMP
	5	JUMP TO THREE in a suit or notrump
TWO NOTRUMP	**4** or less	*Do Not Pass* SHOW a rebiddable *major* suit or any new suit. Otherwise, BID THREE NOTRUMP
	4½ or more	*Try for a slam* by bidding three in a suit (forcing) or RAISE TO FOUR NOTRUMP
For Rebids When Partner Raises See Next Page		
Over Partner's Jump Forcing Takeout		*Do Not Pass. Do not make a jump rebid.* SHOW a new biddable suit REBID a rebiddable suit RAISE with Adequate Support Otherwise, BID NOTRUMP

* But do not "reverse"—page 17.

19

REBIDS WHEN PARTNER RAISES
When to Count Winners

When you or your partner is to be the declarer at a trump contract, you can estimate the total number of tricks you can win by *counting winners* (The Culbertson Distributional Count), which should be used:

1. To know how high to bid when a major suit has been bid and raised.

2. For all sacrifice and defensive bidding (pages 30–37).

3. For opening two-bids (page 27).

OVER PARTNER'S SINGLE RAISE

You may pass. In general, make some rebid with 4 or more honor-tricks. With a 5-card major suit which has been raised, 3½ honor-tricks are enough.

It is more accurate to *count your winners* and with

> 5 winners or less, pass
> 5½ to 6½ winners, bid three
> 7 winners or more, bid four

A rebid of two notrump, or of three in a new suit, is equivalent to bidding three in the raised suit.

You opened one spade. Partner raised to two spades. Your rebid:

1. ♠ A-K-6-5 ♡ Q-7-3 ◇ A-8-5-2 ♣ 8-4 Pass
2. ♠ Q-J-7-5-4 ♡ A-K-2 ◇ A-7-3 ♣ 7-5 Three spades
3. ♠ A-J-8-4-2 ♡ A-7-6 ◇ K-Q-6-4 ♣ 3 Three diamonds
4. ♠ K-Q-10-8-6-4 ♡ A-3 ◇ K-J-7-3 ♣ 2 Four spades

OVER PARTNER'S DOUBLE RAISE

Do not pass unless the contract, because of a part-score, is enough for game.

BID THREE NOTRUMP only with 4-3-3-3 or 4-4-3-2 distribution and a near-minimum hand.

If your suit is a minor, prefer to show a new *major* suit if you have one; or bid three notrump.

Otherwise, bid FOUR in your suit.

Any bid in a new suit is a slam try. Try for a slam with 4 or more honor-tricks (page 44).

You opened one heart. Partner raised to three hearts. Your rebid:

1. ♠ K-6 ♡ A-J-6-2 ◇ K-8-5-4 ♣ Q-J-7 Three notrump
2. ♠ 8-2 ♡ K-8-7-5-4 ◇ A-K-Q-4 ♣ Q-3 Four hearts
3. ♠ A ♡ K-Q-8-5-2 ◇ Q-6-3 ♣ A-Q-6-4 Four clubs

If partner gave a triple raise (page 15) PASS unless, with 5 or more honor-tricks, you can make a slam try.

HOW TO COUNT WINNERS

THE ORIGINAL SUIT-BIDDER COUNTS

1. Honor-winners instead of honor-tricks, thus:

A-K-Q	3	A-J-10	1½	K-J-x	1
A-K-J	2½	Q-J alone	½	Q-J-10	1
A-Q-J	2½	K-Q-J	2	Q-10-x	½
A-Q-10	2	K-Q-10	1½	J-10-x	½

With solid 4-card combinations, add one winner to the value of the 3-card combinations given above. *A-K-J-10 is 3½ honor-winners; Q-J-10-9 is 2 honor-winners, etc.*

Other high cards count as winners at their honor-trick value only, but add a plus value for an uncounted Jack or 10; as in K-10-x, A-J, etc.

In partner's bid suit count one full winner for Ace, King or Q-J; ½ winner for Queen or J-10.

2. Long suits, four cards (J-x-x-x or better) or any longer suit, unless bid by an opponent.

═ WINNERS IN LONG SUITS ═

In Own Trump Suit (if Supported)	Length of Suit	In any Side Suit or in Partner's Suit
1 winner	4 cards	½ winner
2 winners	5 cards	1 winner
3 winners	6 cards	2 winners
4 winners	7 cards	4 winners

Add honor and length winners together for the total trick-winning value of the opening hand.

COUNT IN SUPPORT OF PARTNER'S SUIT

1. Honor-winners as explained above.
2. Long suits, according to the table above.
3. Ruffing tricks, as follows:

═ RUFFING WINNERS ═

With two short suits, count only one—the shorter	With 3 trumps	With 4 or more trumps
Doubleton	½ trick	1 trick
Singleton	1 trick	2 tricks
Void	2 tricks	3 tricks

The full trick-winning value of a singleton or void is included in the ruffing table.

Add honor, length and ruffing winners together for the total supporting value of the hand.

REBIDS BY THE RESPONDER

Situation: Your partner made an opening one-bid in a suit. You made some non-jump response. Your partner has now rebid his hand.

PARTNER'S REBID	If You Hold	YOUR REBID SHOULD BE
ONE OR TWO* IN A NEW SUIT	**1**	PASS, or SHOW PREFERENCE
	1½	RAISE a major with 4 trumps REBID a 6-card suit at *two* only Bid ONE NOTRUMP or SHOW PREFERENCE
	2	REBID your suit or a new suit RAISE with strong trump support*
	2½	BID THREE in a suit or TWO NOTRUMP or raise partner's suit to THREE
TWO NOTRUMP As a jump rebid or as a raise of a 1 NT response	**1+** or less	PASS. Exception: Rebid a 6-card major suit
	1½ or more	REBID a rebiddable major suit SHOW Adequate Support for partner's original suit SHOW a new biddable suit Lacking these values, BID THREE NOTRUMP
TWO NOTRUMP As a non-jump rebid	**1½** or less	REBID a 6-card suit, or SHOW support for partner's suit
	2 or more	JUMP to FOUR in a strong 6-card major suit SHOW a new biddable suit SHOW support for partner's suit, if a major. Otherwise, BID THREE NOTRUMP

* See also Reverse Bidding (page 17). If partner's second suit is higher-ranking than his first suit, do not raise without 4 trumps

PART- NER'S REBID	If You Hold	YOUR REBID SHOULD BE
A JUMP TO THREE In his original suit	**1** or less	RAISE a major with Adequate Support BID THREE, if able, in a rebiddable major suit Otherwise, PASS
	1½ or more	RAISE a major with x-x or better SHOW a rebiddable or new biddable suit at *three* only Otherwise, BID THREE NO-TRUMP
	2½	TRY FOR A SLAM (page 44)
A RAISE In your suit		BID NOTRUMP or rebid a *major* suit with about 2½ honor-tricks (or 1½-2 honor-tricks with 4½ *winners*—page 21) Otherwise, PASS
A JUMP RAISE In your suit	**1** or less	BID FOUR in a 5-card major Otherwise, PASS
	1½ or more	BID FOUR in a major suit Otherwise, BID THREE NO-TRUMP. Three notrump may also bebid with a 4-card major suit and balanced distribution
	2½ or more	TRY FOR A SLAM (page 44)
A FORCING REBID or any other forcing bid	DO NOT PASS	REBID a rebiddable suit RAISE partner's suit with Adequate Support (but do not raise a minor suit to four except as a slam try) SHOW a new biddable suit (but do not bid as high as four in a minor, except as a slam try) Otherwise, BID NOTRUMP

23

page 8
know the
bable
ength of
rtner's suits
m the order
which he
s them. See
o Reverse
ls on page 17

HOW TO SHOW PREFERENCE

When your partner has bid two suits, you *must* (unless an opponent's bid intervenes) show partner *which suit you can best support.*

WHEN PARTNER HAS BID TWO SUITS

Holding	What to Do
Same length in each of partner's suits	*Usually,* PREFER THE SUIT HE BID FIRST
Greater length in one of partner's suits	PREFER THAT SUIT

Thus, if partner has bid first spades and then hearts and you have ♠ A-Q and ♡ 4-3-2, *prefer hearts.* Length is much more important than high cards. But with ♠ 4-3-2 and ♡ A-Q-6, *prefer spades,* the first-bid suit.

If you cannot raise either suit, *or rebid,* then
   PASS if you prefer the second-bid suit (unless partner's rebid was *forcing*—pages 10–11)
   RETURN to the first-bid suit if you prefer it

If your hand *does* justify a raise,
   RAISE ONE TRICK in the second-bid suit, or
   JUMP ONE TRICK in the first-bid suit.

SOUTH	NORTH	North should bid three hearts with:
1 ♠	2 ♣	♠ 6-3 ♡ 8-7-5-2 ◇ A-5 ♣ K-Q-7-4-3
2 ♡		He should bid three (not two) spades with:
		♠ 8-7-5-2 ♡ 6-3 ◇ A-5 ♣ K-Q-7-4-3

If partner's second-bid suit is *higher-ranking* than his first suit, *do not raise it without 4 trumps,* unless he rebids it. (See "Reverse Bidding," page 17).

"Sign-off" Bids

Usually, *the best sign-off is a pass.* But, to take out a dangerous two-notrump contract into a safe 6-card suit, *rebid the suit* to warn partner against notrump *in these situations only:*

SOUTH	WEST	NORTH	EAST	
1 N T	Pass	2 ♠	Pass	North has a very weak hand with a 6-card or longer suit, and asks South to pass.
2 N T	Pass	3 ♠		

SOUTH	WEST	NORTH	EAST	
1 ♠	Pass	2 ♣	Pass	North's three-club rebid shows a hand weak in honor-tricks (1½ or less) with a long club suit.
2 N T	Pass	3 ♣		

24

OPENING ONE-NOTRUMP BIDS

Bid one notrump in any position, vulnerable or not vulnerable, holding

3½ to 4 honor-tricks (never more)

STOPPERS in at least three suits

4-3-3-3 distribution (4-4-3-2 if the doubleton is K-x or better)

Examples of proper opening one-notrump bids:
1. ♠ A-Q-6 ♡ A-8-5-4 ◇ K-Q-6 ♣ 10-7-5 One notrump
2. ♠ J-10-6-5 ♡ A-J ◇ A-Q-7 ♣ A-8-5-3 One notrump

Rarely, bid one notrump on 5-3-3-2 hands if the long suit is a strong *minor* and every suit is stopped:
3. ♠ K-6 ♡ Q-J-8 ◇ A-K-Q-6-4 ♣ Q-6-3 One notrump

With 4 honor-tricks in *two* suits, but lacking a biddable suit:
4. ♠ A-K-6 ♡ A-K-5 ◇ 8-6-4-3 ♣ 9-8-2 One notrump

For openin[g]
Suit-bids s[ee]
page 7. F[or]
higher open[ing]
Notrump b[ids]
see page 27
For Rebids [after]
bidding one [?]
notrump see
next page

NOTRUMP BIDDING

═══RESPONSES TO NOTRUMP BIDS═══	
HOLDING	**PROPER RESPONSE**
1 or less	BID any 6-card or longer suit. Bid a 5-card suit with a 5-5 two-suiter. Otherwise, PASS
1½	BID any 5-card or longer suit Otherwise, PASS
2	RAISE to TWO NOTRUMP or JUMP to FOUR in a 6-card major or bid THREE in a 5-card major suit with unbalanced distribution *Do Not Pass* or bid *two* in a suit
3	RAISE to THREE NOTRUMP or JUMP to THREE (forcing) in a 5-card biddable suit
4 or more	JUMP to THREE in a biddable suit, or bid FOUR NOTRUMP

Proper responses, partner having opened one notrump:
1. ♠ K-Q-7-3-2 ♡ 8-4 ◇ J-7-3 ♣ 6-5-2 Pass
2. ♠ 8-7 ♡ K-J-10-6-5-3 ◇ 6-2 ♣ 6-5-2 Two hearts
3. ♠ Q-6-5 ♡ K-J-3 ◇ A-7 ♣ 8-6-5-3-2 Two notrump
4. ♠ A-K-7-6-5 ♡ 9-6 ◇ A-7 ♣ 9-6-4-3 Three spades
5. ♠ 6-5 ♡ 8-4-3 ◇ A-K-7-6-2 ♣ 8-4-3 Two notrump

ning one-
ump bids
responses
preceding

The Opening Bid Was One Notrump	
THE RESPONSE WAS	**OPENING HAND SHOULD NOW**

A RAISE TO TWO NOTRUMP	*Bid Three Notrump with*
	   a. 3½+honor-tricks or more;
	   b. A stopper in every suit, even with only 3½ honor-tricks PASS only a bare minimum.
	Bid three notrump, holding:
	♠ A-10-6 ♡ K-8-4-3 ◇ A-Q-7 ♣ K-8-5
	♠ A-J-8 ♡ A-Q-4 ◇ A-8-7-3 ♣ 9-5-4
	Pass, holding:
	♠ A-Q-9 ♡ A-6-5 ◇ 8-5-3-2 ♣ A-7-6

A RAISE TO THREE NOTRUMP	Always PASS
TWO IN A SUIT	PASS, lacking 4 honor-tricks. *If you have 4 honor-tricks,* Bid TWO NOTRUMP or RAISE with A-K-x, A-Q-x or K-Q-x in partner's suit. (Raise a *major* with any 4 trumps and a doubleton.) *Partner responded two hearts. Pass with:* ♠ A-Q-9 ♡ 9-6-2 ◇ K-J-7-3 ♣ A-J-6 *Bid two notrump, holding:* ♠ K-Q-4 ♡ 10-8-7 ◇ A-Q-4-3 ♣ A-Q-6 ♠ A-10-9 ♡ K-9-8 ◇ A-6-5-3 ♣ A-Q-5 *Bid three hearts, holding:* ♠ Q-10-4 ♡ A-K-6 ◇ K-9-4-3 ♣ A-J-2

THREE IN A SUIT (FORCING)	DO NOT PASS
	Raise a major suit with 4 trumps
	Bid *three* in a 4-card major, *or*
	BID THREE NOTRUMP
	Partner having bid three clubs:
	♠ K-10-9-5 ♡ A-7-6 ◇ A-Q-5 ♣ Q-J-6
	                    Three spades
	Partner having bid three hearts:
	♠ Q-10-7 ♡ J-10-8-6 ◇ A-K-5-3 ♣ A-Q
	                    Four hearts

FOUR IN A SUIT	Always PASS

STRONG NOTRUMP OPENINGS

Opening suit two-bids on page 28. Higher opening suit-bids on pages 31-32

TWO NOTRUMP

An opening bid of two notrump is *preferred* to an opening one-bid or two-bid on hands with

5 to 6 honor-tricks

including at least A-x, K-10-x, Q-10-x-x or better in *every* suit, and

4-3-3-3 or 4-4-3-2 distribution

A hand with only 5 honor-tricks should include 8 or more honor-cards.

Examples:

♠ K-Q-7-6 ♡ A-K-J ◇ K-J-9 ♣ A-J-7 Two notrump
♠ A-Q ♡ A-K-9-6 ◇ K-Q-J-9 ♣ K-10-8 Two notrump

NOTRUMP BIDDING

RESPONSES TO TWO NOTRUMP

With less than ½ honor-trick, show a 6-card major suit if you have one. Lacking one, pass.

With exactly ½ honor-trick, bid any 5-card or longer suit, but lacking one, pass.

With more than ½ honor-trick, raise to three notrump or show a 5-card biddable suit.

With 2 honor-tricks, try for a slam.

OPENING 3, 4, 5, NOTRUMP BIDS

An opening bid of three or more in notrump is a slam try and is always made on 4-3-3-3 distribution.

THREE NOTRUMP SHOWS
7 to 7½ honor-tricks. Raise once for every top honor (Queen or better) over two, or with 1½ honor tricks. Bid four on Q-x-x-x (5 cards) or better, or any 6-card suit.

FOUR NOTRUMP SHOWS
8 honor-tricks with 10 sure winners. Raise once for every Queen, King or Ace in your hand. Bid five in any 5-card or longer suit.

Five notrump as an opening bid shows 11 sure winners; six notrump shows 12 sure winners. Either of these bids may be raised once for any Queen, King or Ace in the hand.

FORCING TWO-BIDS

The opening bid of two in a suit is the strongest bid in bridge. It is very dangerous to make a forcing two-bid unless your hand surely fulfills the requirements.

After either partner opens with a forcing two-bid, both partners must keep the bidding open until game is reached (unless a penalty double has been made).

The New Rule of 13

WHEN TO MAKE A FORCING TWO-BID

Count your honor-tricks (page 4). Unless you have 4½ or more, you should not make a two-bid no matter how strong your hand. Usually 5 or more are needed.

Count your winners (page 21).

Add your honor-tricks to your winners.

If the total is 13 or more, you may open with two in a biddable suit.

With rare exceptions, the two-bid suit should be headed by A-K or K-Q-J or better.

COUNT OF WINNERS

The method of counting winners was given on page 21. Do not forget to count your honor-tricks at their full value, as shown on page 21. Count the trump suit and side suits the same for length—½ for a 4-card suit, 1 for a 5-card suit, 2 for a 6-card suit, 4 for a 7-card suit. Do not count any value for a singleton as a winner.

EXAMPLES OF SOUND TWO-BIDS

1.	2.	3.
♠ K-Q-J-8-6-4	♠ A-Q-6	♠ A-K-3
♡ A-K	♡ A-K-9-8-6-5	♡ A-K-5
♢ A-K-8	♢ A-K	♢ 5-4
♣ 6-2	♣ 4-3	♣ A-K-J-8-6
8 winners	7½ winners	7½ winners
5 + honor-tricks	5½ honor-tricks	6 honor-tricks
Total 13	Total 13	Total 13½
Bid two spades	Bid two hearts	Bid two clubs

RESPONSES TO TWO-BIDS

A forcing two-bid is forcing even with a part-score (page 41)

When your partner opens with a forcing two-bid DO NOT PASS (unless the intervening opponent overcalls). Choose your response as follows:

IF YOU HOLD	PROPER RESPONSE IS
1 honor-trick or less and no biddable suit as good as x-x-x-x-x-x (6 cards) or Q-J-x-x-x or K-x-x-x-x (5 cards)	TWO NOTRUMP A negative response which denies strength.
Any 6-card suit; or a 5-card suit as good as Q-J-x-x-x or K-x-x-x-x	BID YOUR SUIT
Adequate Trump Support and about 1 honor-trick or more	SINGLE RAISE
Strong Trump Support (x-x-x-x-x or Q-x-x-x) but no Ace, King, singleton or void in the hand	DOUBLE RAISE A warning limit bid, showing trump support but nothing else.
1 + honor-trick	BID ANY BIDDABLE SUIT or raise if able.
1½ honor-tricks	BID ANY BIDDABLE SUIT or BID THREE NOTRUMP
2½ honor-tricks	BID FOUR NOTRUMP* but prefer to show a biddable suit first.
3 honor-tricks or more	BID FIVE NOTRUMP* but prefer to show a biddable suit first.

FORCING TWO-BIDS

* These bids are forcing but not conventional (pages 46–47).

SACRIFICE BIDDING

Making a game often has an invisible value which does not show on the score sheet. This is because it increases the chance of winning the rubber.

The First Game to either side has a TOTAL value of	about	**400**	points
Winning a Second Straight Game has an actual value of	about	**500**	points
The Rubber Game (when both sides are vulnerable) is worth	about	**600**	points

Therefore it is always profitable to overbid and go down 300 points or less *when you are sure the opponents can make a game*. But never go down more than 500 points to prevent an opposing game.

THE RULE OF TWO AND THREE

When the opponents are bidding, and partner has passed or has made no bid, do not bid unless you can win, in your own hand,

Within **2** tricks of your contract if VULNERABLE

Within **3** tricks of your contract if NOT VULNERABLE

Then you will never be set more than 500 points. This Rule of Two and Three governs all defenders' bids (pages 33–35) and all sacrifice bidding. When partner *has* bid (or raised) count your combined winners (page 21) to decide on whether to make a sacrifice overbid or not.

For a *profitable* sacrifice your combined hands should promise within one trick of your contract if vulnerable; within two tricks if not vulnerable. A three- or four-trick set, respectively, is justified to keep your opponents from making a slam.

OPENING THREE-BIDS

An opening bid of three in a suit is often a *weaker* bid than an opening one-bid. Its purpose is to shut out the opponents and also to show a strong trump suit. It requires:

A defender's overall of three does not necessarily show such a strong suit —see page 34

A SOLID 6-CARD OR LONGER SUIT

In a minor
A-K-Q-J-x-x
A-K-Q-x-x-x-x
or better

In a major
K-Q-J-10-x-x
K-Q-J-x-x-x-x
or better

AT LEAST 6, AT MOST 7½ WINNERS
NO MORE THAN 1 OUTSIDE HONOR-TRICK

Under the Rule of 2 & 3 (page 30) a *vulnerable* three-bid should have 7 winners or more.

Examples, vulnerable or not vulnerable:
1. ♠ K-Q-J-10-8-5-2   ♡ 7   ◇ K-J-6   ♣ 8-3   Three spades
2. ♠ 8-3   ♡ 9   ◇ A-K-Q-J-6-5   ♣ J-10-8-3   Three diamonds

Examples, only if not vulnerable:
1. ♠ K-Q-J-10-8-6   ♡ 7   ◇ 6-3-2   ♣ Q-J-10   Three spades
2. ♠ 3-2   ♡ A-Q-J-10-6-5   ◇ K-7-4   ♣ 5-4   Three hearts

OPENING SUIT 3, 4, 5 BIDS

Responses to Opening Three-bids

1. **RAISE** a major-suit three-bid to four with 2½ winners. These must be honor-tricks or ruffing winners (page 21). A raise of a minor-suit three-bid requires 3½ winners, but prefer three notrump.

2. **BID THREE NOTRUMP** with 1½ honor-tricks in two suits. (The three-bidder, however, should then return to four of his suit if it is not absolutely solid.)

3. **BID THREE** in a strong rebiddable major suit (when the three-bid was in a minor) with about 2½ honor-tricks.

Any other response is a slam try (page 44) and requires at least 3½ honor-tricks including two Aces.

Partner opens with three spades. Holding:
♠ 6-3   ♡ Q-8-4-2   ◇ Q-6-2   ♣ A-7-5-4   Three notrump
♠ 6-4-2   ♡ 9   ◇ A-Q-6-3   ♣ 9-7-6-3-2   Four spades

Partner opens with three clubs. Holding:
♠ J-10-8-6   ♡ Q-6-2   ◇ A-K-Q-4-3   ♣ 3   Three notrump
♠ K-Q-10-8-5-4   ♡ 9-7-6   ◇ A-J-10   ♣ 8   Three spades

The best defense against opponents' three-bids is the optional double (page 36).

31

These bids are
based on the
"Sacrifice
Principle"—
page 30. See
also the Count
of Winners—
page 21

SHUT-OUT (PREËMPTIVE) BIDS

An opening bid of four in *any* suit, or five in a *minor*, shows a powerful trump suit but great *weakness* in honor-tricks. Such a bid is an intentional sacrifice overbid (page 30).

Shut-out bids are highly effective and should be used whenever available. But no shut-out overbid should ever be made fourth hand after three passes.

AN OPENING FOUR-BID REQUIRES

A strong 7-card, or any 8-card suit

About **8** winners if NOT VULNERABLE, but *sure* winners if VULNERABLE

No more than 2+ honor-tricks in the hand

FOR A MINOR-SUIT FIVE-BID

An 8-card or longer trump suit

About **9** winners if NOT VULNERABLE, but *sure* winners if VULNERABLE

No more than 2+ honor-tricks in the hand

Examples:

♠ Q-J-10-8-7-6-5-2 ♡ 6 ◇ K-Q-J ♣ 5 Four spades
♠ 6 ♡ 5-2 ◇ 8 ♣ A-K-9-8-7-6-5-3-2 Five clubs

Raises of Shut-out Bids

DO NOT RAISE partner's major-suit four-bid or minor-suit five-bid unless there is an intervening bid, or unless you want to try for a slam.

IF THE OPPONENTS BID A GAME, raise partner's suit ONCE with 2 winners, TWICE with 3 winners, etc. The winners must be honor-tricks or supporting trump tricks (page 21). However, no trump support is required to raise.

TRY FOR A SLAM only if you have 4 honor-tricks including three Aces; or two Aces plus the King or Queen of partner's suit.

RAISE a minor-suit four-bid to five (game) with 3 honor-tricks, or 2 honor-tricks plus one supporting trump trick.

IN DOUBLING an opponent's bid, *do not depend upon partner for any defensive tricks after he has made an opening shut-out bid.*

BIDS BY THE DEFENDERS

When an opponent opens the bidding, you may count at least 3 honor-tricks against you. Before entering the bidding, your first thought is *safely*. (See page 30, The Rule of 2 & 3). Nevertheless, you may wish to bid:

(a) For defensive purposes: To interfere with the opponents' bidding, to find a profitable sacrifice (page 30) or to tell partner the best suit to lead;

(b) For aggressive purposes, when your hand is strong enough to make a contract of your own.

Nearly all Defenders' bidding is based on the Culbertson Rule of Two and Three— page 30

HOLDING	YOU SHOULD
1 to **2** honor-tricks	MAKE A SHUT-OUT BID of four or five if able (page 32) OVERCALL in a strong 5-card or longer suit *if you have enough winners* (page 21)
2½ to **3** honor-tricks	OVERCALL if able (page 34) Rarely, make a takeout double (page 36)
3½ to **4** honor-tricks	TAKEOUT DOUBLE (page 36) JUMP OVERCALL (page 35) BID ONE NOTRUMP (page 25) provided you have a sure stopper in the opponents' suit
4½ or more honor-tricks	*Usually*, TAKEOUT DOUBLE But if you would be almost strong enough for an opening forcing two-bid (page 28), you may OVERCALL IN THE OPPONENTS' SUIT (page 35) BID FOUR (or five) NOTRUMP over opponents' preëmptive bid.

DEFENDERS' BIDDING

With strong hands prefer Takeout Doubles— page 36

DEFENDERS' OVERCALLS

When the opponents open the bidding, count your winners (page 21) before deciding on an overcall.

OVERCALL	AT ONE-ODD	AT TWO-ODD
WHEN *NOT* VULNER-ABLE	**4** winners **AND** **1½** honor-tricks with a 5- or 6-card suit **2** or more honor-tricks with a 4-card suit	**5** winners **AND** **1½** honor-tricks with a 6-card suit **2** honor-tricks with a rebiddable suit
WHEN YOU ARE VULNER-ABLE	**5** *sure* winners **AND** **1½** honor-tricks with a 6-card suit **2** honor-tricks with a rebiddable suit Avoid 4-card suits	**6** *sure* winners **AND** **2** honor-tricks with a 6-card or a strong 5-card suit (A-Q-x-x-x, etc.)

When a bid of three is required to overcall, the hand must contain 6 sure winners if not vulnerable and 7 sure winners if vulnerable, and the trump suit should be a 6-card or longer suit. An honor-trick holding of 1½–2 is sufficient.

When not vulnerable, a 6-card or longer suit may be bid with slightly less than 1½ honor-tricks if the required winners are held.

Responses to Overcalls

TO RAISE partner's overcall you need

1 ½ or more honor-tricks

X-X-X (any three or more trumps) to support a suit in which partner bids *two* or *three*.

Count your supporting winners (page 21). You may raise once for each winner over 2 if vulnerable; for each winner over 3 if not vulnerable.

TAKE OUT in a suit or notrump with 2 or more honor-tricks, but do not count on partner for more than 1½ tricks in support of your bid.

MAKE A JUMP SUIT TAKEOUT (*one-round forcing*) with 2½ to 3 honor-tricks including a strong suit of your own or support for partner's suit.

STRENGTH SHOWING OVERCALLS

See Slam
Bidding on
pages 44-47

THE JUMP OVERCALL

A jump overcall (one trick more than necessary) of an opponent's opening bid shows

> 3 or more honor-tricks, usually $3\frac{1}{2}$
> Two 5-card or longer suits; or
> One long, strong major suit, with 8 winners

An opponent opens with one diamond. Proper overcall:
1. ♠ A-K-10-5-4 ♡ A-Q-J-7-5 ◇ 6 ♣ 3-2 Two spades
2. ♠ K-Q-J-8-7-5-3 ♡ A-6 ◇ A-5-3 ♣ 4 Two spades

An opponent opens with one spade. Proper overcall:
♠ 6 ♡ A-K-10-9-8-7-5 ◇ A-J-10 ♣ K-9 Three hearts

RAISE a jump overcall with about **1 honor-trick** or more and x-x-x or better in trumps;

BID NOTRUMP with **1+ honor-trick** or more;

TAKE OUT in a rebiddable *major* suit or in any strong rebiddable suit with $1\frac{1}{2}$ or more honor-tricks.

A NOTRUMP OVERCALL

An overcall of an opponent's one-bid with *one notrump* is the same as an opening one-notrump bid (page 25) but must include one stopper, and preferably a double stopper, in the opponents' suit.

Partner responds as to an opening one-notrump bid (page 25).

FORCING OVERCALLS

When an opponent opens the bidding and your hand would almost justify an *opening* two-bid (page 28) overcall by bidding the opponent's suit. This overcall must be made at your first opportunity.

Over an opponent's opening one-club bid, force to game:
1. ♠ K-Q-10-6 ♡ A-K-Q-5-4 ◇ K-J-10-6 ♣ — Two clubs
2. ♠ A-K-Q-10-5-4-2 ♡ A-Q-J ◇ K-Q ♣ 3 Two clubs

This overcall usually shows at least second-round control (page 44) in the opponents' suit.

When the opponent's bid is a preëmptive four-bid, such a hand is shown by bidding FOUR NOTRUMP (not an ace-showing slam try); when the opponents' bid is a preëmptive five-bid, the proper overcall is FIVE NOTRUMP.

All these bids are gigantic takeout doubles. Partner responds by showing his best suit.

See also the "Forcing Overcall" and 4-5 Notrump Overcalls on page 35

THE TAKEOUT DOUBLE

A double is intended to be taken out only when

1. Partner has made no bid (or double)*;
2. It is made at the doubler's first opportunity;
3. The doubled bid is one, two or three in a suit.

A player who has opened the bidding with *one in a suit* may later make a takeout double of his opponents' bid, or a defender may *repeat* his takeout double; if the situation conforms to *all three* requirements.

REQUIREMENTS FOR TAKEOUT DOUBLES

A takeout double requires a very strong hand:

3 honor-tricks (usually more) and either
Strong support for every unbid suit; or
A rebiddable suit in the hand and at least 6 sure winners.

Examples, opponent having bid one diamond:
1. ♠ Q-J-6-3   ♡ 10-9-5-2   ◇ K-6   ♣ A-K-8   Double
2. ♠ A-6-5   ♡ K-Q-8-6-4   ◇ 2   ♣ A-7-4-3   Double
3. ♠ A-K-J-8-6-4   ♡ J-7-6-2   ◇ A   ♣ 4-3   Double

A DOUBLE OF ONE NOTRUMP

A double of one notrump is a penalty double, but in certain cases the doubler's partner should take out (see next page).

OPTIONAL DOUBLES of Preëmptive Bids

A double of an opponent's opening three-bid shows 4 honor-tricks; a double of an opponent's opening four-bid shows 3½ honor-tricks; and in either case the doubler guarantees Adequate Trump Support (J-10-x, Q-x-x or better) in every unbid suit.

The doubler's partner should *take out* with 1½ to 2 honor-tricks plus a 5-card biddable suit (slightly less with a 6-card suit) but should otherwise pass for penalties.

REOPENING THE BIDDING

When an opposing opening *suit-bid* is passed by the opener's partner, a takeout double by fourth hand may be shaded to 2 honor-tricks.

---

* A *penalty pass* (see next page) is equivalent to a penalty double.

HOW TO TAKE OUT A DOUBLE

When your partner makes a takeout double and the next player passes, you must respond. *The weaker your hand, the greater the obligation to bid.*

You do not pass a Takeout Double for Penalties without at least 4 sure Trump Tricks. But see also Penalty Doubles on pages 42-43

WHEN THE DOUBLED BID IS IN A SUIT	IF YOU HOLD	WHEN THE DOUBLED BID IS NOTRUMP
BID your longest unbid suit. With suits of equal length, bid the one which can be shown at the lowest level	Less than 1 H. T.	BID a 5-card or longer suit. Otherwise, PASS (Making the contract will not give the opponents game. But take out in your best suit if an opponent redoubles)
BID your best suit (prefer a major) or BID ONE NO-TRUMP with 1½ honor-tricks; even without the opponents' suit stopped	1 to 1½ H. T.	PASS for penalties. (But if *all* your strength is in one 5-card or longer suit, bid the suit. With 1½ tricks in a 6-card suit, jump to three.)
JUMP one trick in your best suit (prefer a major) or BID TWO NO-TRUMP with a double stopper in the opponents' suit	2 or more H. T.	PASS. Only exception: Freak distribution which makes a game almost sure, in which case jump to three in a contract.

TAKEOUT DOUBLES

After An Intervening Bid
OR A REDOUBLE OF A DOUBLED SUIT-BID

PASS a worthless hand.

BID a 6-card suit. Bid a 5-card suit with about ½ to 1 honor-trick.

BID any biddable suit with 1 to 2 honor-tricks.

JUMP ONE TRICK in a biddable suit with more than 2 honor-tricks.

But a pass of a redoubled one-notrump bid is a *penalty pass* and is made in accordance with the requirements given in the table above.

FREE RESPONSES

When partner makes an opening one-bid
and the intervening opponent overcalls,

DO NOT RAISE without 1½ honor-tricks. With
2 honor-tricks and no available suit or notrump bid,
raise (single raise only) with as little trump support
as x-x-x.

DO NOT MAKE a one-over-one bid without 2
honor-tricks (1½ with a 6-card suit).

DO NOT BID ONE NOTRUMP without 2
honor-tricks including at least one stopper (preferably a double stopper) in the opponents' suit.

DO NOT BID TWO IN A SUIT without 2 honor-
tricks, and if your suit is higher-ranking than partner's, or if you must bid *three* to show it, you must
have 2½ honor-tricks.

Otherwise, respond as indicated on pages 12 to 16.
See also Penalty Doubles and particularly Light
Doubles (pages 42–43).

Partner bids one club.   Opponent bids one heart.
♠ A-10-8-5-3   ♡ 7-6-4   ◇ Q-9-5   ♣ 8-6   Pass
♠ K-Q-7-6   ♡ 7-5-4   ◇ Q-J-4-3   ♣ K-8   One spade
♠ 9-8-6   ♡ K-J-3   ◇ A-7-6-2   ♣ Q-J-4   One notrump
♠ A-7   ♡ 7-6-4   ◇ 9-7-5-3   ♣ A-7-4-2   Two clubs

When Partner's Bid is Doubled

When an opponent makes a takeout double of
partner's opening one-bid *in a suit*, a bid by you
denies strength. It is intended chiefly to make it
difficult for the doubler's partner to respond.

REDOUBLE, to show a strong hand, with 2 or
more honor-tricks, with or without trump support.

PASS with 1½ to 2 bare honor-tricks. *But also
pass a worthless hand.*

RAISE TWICE (a weak preëmptive raise) with
4 or more trumps and about 5 supporting winners;
raise *once* with 3 winners; regardless of honor-tricks.

MAKE A JUMP SUIT TAKEOUT (forcing for
one round only) with a strong hand (more than 2
honor-tricks) and freak distribution.

Partner bids one heart.   Opponent doubles.
♠ 7-6   ♡ Q-7-4-2   ◇ K-8-5-4   ♣ 9-4-3   Two hearts
♠ 7   ♡ Q-10-6-5   ◇ 10-9-6-5   ♣ K-J-4-3   Three hearts
♠ A-10-5-3   ♡ 7-6   ◇ K-J-8-6   ♣ Q-7-6   Redouble
♠ 10-9-2   ♡ —   ◇ A-K-Q-8-7-6-3   ♣ K-8-2   Three diamonds

38

FREE REBIDS BY THE OPENER

Requirements for rebids on pages 17-24.

When Partner Has Responded

Situation: You have made an opening one-bid in a suit; partner has responded; the intervening opponent has overcalled. *Even if partner's response was forcing, you may pass.* Any rebid you make now is a *free* rebid and shows that you had more than a minimum bid. If your opening bid was based on:

3 honor-tricks or less — MAKE a free rebid only on a strong 6-card or a 7-card suit or to show a 5-5 two-suiter. Do not in any case bid more than two in a suit. RAISE ONCE with four trumps in support of partner's suit, if a major. Otherwise, PASS.

3½ honor-tricks — MAKE a free rebid in a 6-card suit or a *new* 5-card suit *at the level of two.* Bid one (but never two) notrump with a stopper in the opponents' suit. Raise once with Adequate Trump Support.

4 honor-tricks or more — REBID in accordance with pages 18–19. Do not pass except with four *bare* honor-tricks and 4-3-3-3 or 4-4-3-2 distribution. BID NOTRUMP with a stopper in the opponents' suit (a two-notrump rebid requires a double stopper). RAISE with Adequate Trump Support, but a *jump* raise need not be given on minimum requirements as any raise is a free raise and shows extra strength. DO NOT make a free rebid in a *5-card* suit weaker than A-K-x-x-x or Q-J-10-x-x.

FREE BIDS

PENALTY AND TAKEOUT DOUBLES

Any double you make is a *penalty double* (pages 42–43). Do not rely on partner for more than *one* defensive winner unless he made a jump response or a free response (page 38).

If partner's response has been doubled for a take-out, any rebid by you *denies* great strength. *Redouble* with 4 or more honor-tricks.

WHAT PARTNER'S BIDS PROMISE

When your side has opened the bidding, count on partner for *at least* the following honor-tricks. Also use this table to judge your opponents' combined strength when they have opened the bidding.

THE BID	As an Opening Bid	As a Response	As a Rebid by the Opener	As a Rebid by the Responder
One in a suit	2½	1	2½	1½
Two in a suit	5½	2*	3*	2
Three in a suit	1	3½	4	2½
Four in a suit	0	0	4½	2½
One notrump	3½	1	2½	1½
Two notrump	5	3	4	2½
Three notrump	7	4	5	3
Four notrump	8	Conventional (see page 45).		

* Unless it is a jump bid, as 2 ♣ over 1 ♡, in which case it shows about 2 honor-tricks *more*. See also "Reverse Bids," page 17.

WHEN PARTNER PASSES

When you open the bidding, the next player passes and your partner fails to keep the bidding open by making a response to your bid, do not expect him to have anything.

But when partner passes originally, or fails to overcall an opponent's bid, or has not yet bid, he is still likely to have about 1 honor-trick. Use the Rule of 8 (page 5). Add *your* honor-tricks to the honor-tricks the opponents have shown by their bidding; subtract the total from 8. The result may be close to zero, warning you that partner has a blank hand; again, it may show that he is likely to have some undisclosed strength.

WHEN PARTNER MAKES A "FREE BID"

Any "free bid" over an opponent's bid by the *responder* usually shows at least 2 honor-tricks; by the *opener*, at least 3½ honor-tricks (pages 38–39).

See also Defenders' Bidding, pages 33 to 37.

PART-SCORE BIDDING

*See also
Sacrifice
Bidding on
page 30*

When your side has a part-score (20 or more points in the trick-score toward game) the Culbertson System is modified to the following extent:

1. A forcing two-bid, or a forcing takeout or forcing rebid (both of which are *jump* bids in a *new* suit), is still forcing, even though game has been reached. A bid in the opponents' suit is also forcing.

2. Other bids which are usually forcing *may be passed* if a contract sufficient (with the part-score) for game has already been reached.

3. Keep partner's opening one-bid open with about ½ honor-trick *less*, or with *slightly* less trump support (such as 10-x-x) than is usually required. Thus, respond one notrump, or bid *one* in any biddable suit, with slightly less than 1 honor-trick.

4. A one-notrump *response*, if the part-score is 30, 40 or 50, is *forcing* (because the responder can often use it, on strong hands, to trap the opponents into overcalling).

5. Do not open the bidding *fourth hand* with the bare minimum requirements if your principal strength is in the minor suits.

6. An opening preëmptive bid (pages 31-32), even though more than enough for game, is *not* a slam try.

PART-SCORE ✔
BIDDING

WHEN YOUR OPPONENTS HAVE A PART-SCORE

1. Shade the requirements for opening bids to 2½ honor-tricks and a biddable *4-card* suit, as on such hands it would be even more dangerous to overcall later if an opponent opens the bidding.

2. Prefer to open the bidding with one notrump rather than a suit-bid with 4-4-3-2, 5-3-3-2 and even 6-3-2-2 hands, provided the long suit is a minor and you have enough honor-tricks (page 25).

3. Overcall an opponent's opening bid even with no honor-tricks at all if you have enough *winners* (page 34).

See also
Takeout
Doubles on
page 36

PENALTY DOUBLES

A double is for *penalties* (to increase the value of undertrick penalties, in the expectation that the opposing contract will be defeated):

(*a*) *Whenever the doubler's partner has made any bid, double or* penalty pass (*page 37*).

(*b*) *When the doubled bid is in notrump, or is four or more in a suit.*

(*c*) *When the doubler opened with a notrump bid or a bid of two or more in a suit, or*

(*d*) *In any event, if the doubler, at a previous opportunity to make a takeout double, did not do so.*

WHEN TO DOUBLE FOR PENALTIES

1. *The Two-Trick Rule.* You must count enough *defensive winners* in the combined hands to defeat the opponents' contract *at least two tricks.*

2. The expected penalty must be worth more than any contract your side can *surely* bid and make.

3. Even if you can probably make a game, generally prefer to double for penalties when you expect to defeat the opponents 500 points or more.

HOW TO COUNT DEFENSIVE WINNERS

Against the opponents' *trump* contract, count

1. Honor-tricks at their defensive value only (page 4). But in a suit bid by your left-hand opponent, K-x should not be counted at all, and A-Q should be expected to win only one trick.

2. Honor-tricks in partner's hand (as shown by his bidding). See page 40.

3. Trump tricks. This includes any *stopper* in the opponents' suit (J-x-x-x, etc.). *Length* in the opponents' trump suit is more important than high cards.

WHEN TO TAKE OUT A PENALTY DOUBLE

Do not take out partner's penalty double *unless*

(a) The doubled bid is one notrump (page 37) or

(b) You have freak distribution (such as 5-5-3-0, 7-4-1-1, 6-5-1-1, etc.) including a singleton or void in the opponents' suit, *and* you expect to score more points (or to lose fewer points) by playing the hand than by doubling the opponents.

Double ONE NOTRUMP With

4½ or more honor-tricks in the combined hands. Usually the defenders should also have a strong suit to lead. This may be a suit which one partner has bid and for which the other partner has support.

It follows that when a defender doubles an *opening* one-notrump bid, he should have 3½, and usually more, honor-tricks plus some fairly strong suit such as Q-J-10-x, A-K-x-x-x, or better, to open.

For example: ♠ A-8-3   ♡ K-Q-5   ◇ Q-2   ♣ K-Q-J-7-2

Double TWO NOTRUMP With

4 or more honor-tricks *sure* in the combined hands and the strong probability of a stopper in *every* suit. *Only exception:* When the defenders have a long, established suit of their own to lead.

Double THREE NOTRUMP With

4 or more honor-tricks; or a strong suit to open and enough *entries* (including honor-tricks or stoppers in the opponents' bid suits) to establish and win 6 or more tricks.

Decide on the suit to be opened and estimate the number of *stoppers* declarer probably has in that suit. You will need, *in addition to the opening lead*, exactly as many *sure* entries as declarer has stoppers.

See page 58 for proper opening leads against doubled notrump contracts.

LIGHT PENALTY DOUBLES

You may double an opponent's *vulnerable overcall* of *one* in *any* suit, or *two clubs* or *two diamonds* (so that, even if the doubled contract is made, it will not give the opponents game); if:

1. You have about 2½ honor-tricks; and
2. You have Q-x-x or 10-x-x-x, or better, in the opponents' suit.

But do not double with four cards in partner's suit; for fear his honor-tricks will be trumped.

The Light Doubler's partner should take out the double unless he has at least two cards in the opponent's suit; or at least 3½ honor-tricks in three suits.

The finer points of doubles and redoubles are clearly explained in Culbertson's OFFICIAL BOOK

PENALTY DOUBLES

WHEN TO TRY FOR A SLAM

When you are sure you and your partner together have 6½ honor-tricks or more, you *may* be in the slam zone and should check up on the following:

HONOR-TRICKS

Except with freak hands, 7 or more honor-tricks are needed to make a slam. Your opponents then have at most 1½ honor-tricks (page 5). You will have to win a finesse to make your slam.

THE TRUMP SUIT

At least eight trumps in the combined hands, including at least three of the four top honors (A, K and Q; or A, Q and J; or K, Q and J). Unless you have a rebiddable suit which partner has supported, or very strong support such as K-J-x-x for partner's suit (if he has not rebid it), or a solid suit, you cannot be sure of sufficient trump strength.

A SIDE SUIT

In addition to the trump suit, there must usually be a strong, 5-card or longer *side suit* in the hand of one partner. The presence of such a suit is usually apparent when one partner has bid and rebid it, and the other partner has support such as Q-x or J-10.

Without such a side suit, a slam can seldom be made without about 8 honor-tricks.

SUIT CONTROLS

First-round control is a card which will win a trick the first time its suit is led. An ace, or a void suit at trump contracts, is first-round control.

Second-round control is the ability to win the second lead of a suit, after the opponents have won the first lead with the ace. Any king, or at trump contracts a singleton, is second-round control.

For a small slam you must have first-round control in three suits and at least second-round control in the fourth suit. For a grand slam you need first-round control in all four suits; a *solid* combined trump suit; and 13 sure winners.

When you can assume the combined hands to fulfill all these requirements, you may make a slam try.

44

DIRECT SLAM TRIES

Advanced players are advised to learn the Asking Bids —See Culbertson's GOLD BOOK

Conventional slam methods (see pages 46–47) are more accurate than other methods, but with inexperienced partners you should use *direct* slam tries.

A BID OF MORE THAN GAME

An *unnecessary* bid of more than game is a slam invitation (except in some *part-score* situations).

SOUTH	WEST	NORTH	EAST		SOUTH	WEST	NORTH	EAST
1 ♠	Pass	2 ♣	Pass		1 ♠	2 ♦	4 ♠	5 ♦
4 ♠	Pass	5 ♠			Pass	Pass	5 ♠	

Unnecessary bid of more than game—slam try. | *Not a slam try, because necessary to overcall opponents.*

MAKE a slam invitation when all the slam requirements (see opposite page) are *probably* present.

ACCEPT your partner's slam invitation when you have *any* strength (even a plus value, or extra length or strength in the trump suit) which has not been fully disclosed by your previous bids.

However, the partner who has made the stronger bids should generally not make or accept a slam try without at least two aces.

SOUTH	WEST	NORTH	EAST
1 ♠	Pass	2 ♦	Pass
3 ♠	Pass	5 ♠	

North's five-spade bid is a slam invitation. He may hold:

♠ Q-7-2   ♡ 9   ◇ A-K-Q-8-4   ♣ J-7-5-3

South's three-spade bid promised a 6-card suit and (usually) at least 4 honor-tricks. South's action now should be:

1. ♠ A-K-9-6-4-3   ♡ K-Q-6   ◇ 7-5   ♣ K-Q   Pass = only one Ace
2. ♠ A-K-10-6-4-3-2   ♡ A-Q-6   ◇ J-3   ♣ 8   Six spades
3. ♠ A-J-10-6-4-3   ♡ Q-6   ◇ 7-5   ♣ A-8   Six spades
4. ♠ K-J-10-9-8-5   ♡ A-Q   ◇ 6   ♣ A-Q-8-2   Six spades

CONTROL-SHOWING BIDS

A bid in the opponents' suit is a slam try. It guarantees first-round control (ace or void) of that suit, plus very strong support for partner's suit (or a solid trump suit in the bidder's own hand).

SOUTH	WEST	NORTH	EAST		SOUTH	WEST	NORTH	EAST
1 ♡	1 ♠	2 ♠			1 ♡	1 ♠	3 ◇	Pass
					3 ♠			

North has first-round spade control and powerful heart support. *South should respond as to a forcing takeout (page 16).* If South is strong in the spade suit, he should usually respond by bidding notrump.

South has first-round spade control and either powerful diamond support or a powerful heart suit. *North should respond as to any other slam invitation.*

SLAM BIDDING

FOUR NOTRUMP SLAM TRIES

A bid of four notrump, being more than game, is almost invariably used as a slam try.

It is merely a *direct slam invitation* when given as a raise to partner's *opening* notrump bid or to partner's *jump rebid* in notrump.

By prior agreement between partners, and with the knowledge of their opponents, a bid of four notrump may and *should* be used as a *conventional* slam try which requires partner to respond in such a way as to show his Aces and other suit controls.

THE 4-5 NOTRUMP CONVENTION

The Culbertson 4–5 Notrump Convention is superior to all other slam-bidding conventions because (a) the four-notrump bidder himself must show certain values; and (b) voids, as well as Aces, may be shown in responding.

A bid of four notrump by either partner, when a game has been reached or when previous bidding has disclosed slam possibilities (page 44), guarantees that the bidder has in his hand either

(a) Any three Aces; or

(b) Any two Aces plus the King in any suit previously bid by himself or his partner.

He may have *more* than these requirements, but he must not have *less*.

After a conventional four-notrump bid, the bidder's partner *must not pass.* He responds as shown on the next page.

EXAMPLES OF FOUR NOTRUMP BIDS

SOUTH	WEST	NORTH	EAST
1 ♡	Pass	2 ◇	Pass
3 ◇	Pass	4 ♡	Pass
4 N T	*Conventional and forcing*		

South's slam try shows that he has three Aces, or two Aces plus the King of hearts, or diamonds, or both. *South may hold:*

1. ♠ A-6   ♡ K-J-10-8-4   ◇ A-8-5-2   ♣ Q-6
2. ♠ A-6   ♡ A-J-8-6-4   ◇ A-Q-3   ♣ Q-7-3
3. ♠ 9-6   ♡ A-J-8-6-4   ◇ K-Q-3   ♣ A-J-2

SHOWING ALL FOUR ACES

When a player who has previously made a four-notrump slam try later bids five notrump it shows that he holds all four Aces in his hand.

FOUR NOTRUMP SLAM TRIES (Continued)

Advanced players may profit from use of the Asking Bids. See Culbertson's GOLD BOOK

Do not pass partner's conventional four-notrump bid. The following respsonses are *obligatory*.

ANY TWO ACES. Respond *five notrump.*

ONE ACE *plus the Kings of all the suits* which have been previously bid by *either* partner. Respond *five notrump.* Partner, lacking the King of any bid suit, must hold three Aces for his four-notrump bid.

ONE ACE, or a void, in any *unbid* suit. Bid *five* in the suit in which the Ace or void is held. *But with no added values, you may sign off (see below).*

ONE ACE in a suit which has previously been bid; or no Ace, but the Kings of *all* bid suits. *Jump to six* in the best available trump suit, if holding added values; but otherwise *sign off* as explained below.

NO ACE *and no void* (unless you hold the Kings of all bid suits). SIGN OFF. To sign off, you simply bid five in the *lowest* suit which has previously been bid by either partner. This does *not* indicate support for that suit; you *may* have a singleton.

For example:	SOUTH	WEST	NORTH	EAST
	1 ♡	Pass	1 ♠	Pass
	3 ◇	Pass	4 ♡	Pass
	4 N T	Pass		

North's responses are:

1. ♠ A-J-6-3   ♡ A-7-4-2   ◇ Q-7-3   ♣ 8-2   Five notrump
2. ♠ K-Q-7-6-3   ♡ Q-8-4-3   ◇ 6   ♣ K-Q-7   Five diamonds
3. ♠ Q-8-6-4-2   ♡ 10-9-6-4   ◇ 6   ♣ A-J-5   Five clubs
4. ♠ A-7-6-4-3   ♡ 9-8-4-3   ◇ 3   ♣ Q-8-4   Five diamonds
5. ♠ A-K-7-4   ♡ 10-9-6-4   ◇ 3-2   ♣ Q-J-3   Six hearts

THE BLACKWOOD SLAM CONVENTION

In this convention, a player may bid four notrump without any specific strength required in his own hand. His partner *must* then respond as follows:

Five clubs, *lacking* an Ace.
Five diamonds, holding *one* Ace.
Five hearts, holding *two* Aces.
Five spades, holding *three* Aces.
Five notrump, holding *all four* Aces.

4–5 NOTRUMP SLAM BIDS

If, after the four-notrump bid and response, either player bids *five* notrump, his partner must then show Kings on the same schedule of responses, i.e.: six clubs with *no* King, six diamonds with *one* King, six hearts with *two* Kings, six spades with *three* Kings, six notrump with *all four* Kings.

47

*Full chapters
on Duplicate
Bridge methods
in Culbertson's
OFFICIAL
BOOK and
GOLD BOOK*

DUPLICATE BRIDGE METHODS

Most duplicate bridge games are scored by match-points, and in such games your bidding methods should be modified as follows:

1. A vulnerable game made against you will give your opponents 600 to 660 points. You must therefore seek every possible sacrifice contract (page 30). In order to find your best combined trump suit most often, when you are *not* vulnerable and your opponents *are* vulnerable, overcall the opponents' opening bids with *one winner less* than you would require in rubber bridge. When not vulnerable, overcalls, and raises of partner's overcalls, should be based on winners, regardless of honor-tricks (at times with no honor-tricks at all).

2. Prefer to try for a probable vulnerable game rather than double nonvulnerable opponents for a sure 3-trick penalty.

3. Rather than make a doubtful overcall, reduce the requirements for takeout doubles by ½ honor-trick when holding support for all unbid suits.

4. Do not fail to reopen the bidding (when an opening bid is passed) if you have 1½ honor-tricks or more.

5. Seek major- rather than minor-suit contracts, and prefer to play notrump rather than suit slams in order to score the 10 points extra for tricks.

6. If you could make a part-score contract and the opponents overcall it, double them even when you expect to defeat them only one trick.

7. Avoid opening 3- or 4-bids when holding 2 or more honor-tricks. It may be possible to play the hand at a contract of two-odd or three-odd, respectively, and make it.

8. Whereas in rubber bridge you should try for a major-suit game with about 9 winners in the combined hands; and try for a small slam which depends on a successful finesse; stop short of these doubtful contracts in duplicate bridge.

9. Use the *Light Penalty Double* (page 43) as much as possible when your opponents are vulnerable and you are not. Beating them one trick (200 points) is better than any part-score contract you can make.

48

CARD PROBABILITIES

"Percentage Plays" based on Sound Bridge mathematics are explained in Culbertson's OFFICIAL BOOK

SUIT DIVISIONS

If you and your Partner together hold in one suit:	The cards of that suit in your Opponents' hands will be divided:	
6 cards	4-3	62 times in 100 deals
	5-2	31 times in 100 deals
	6-1	7 times in 100 deals
	7-0	Less than 1 time in 200 deals
7 cards	4-2	48 times in 100 deals
	3-3	36 times in 100 deals
	5-1	15 times in 100 deals
	6-0	1 time in 100 deals
8 cards	3-2	68 times in 100 deals
	4-1	28 times in 100 deals
	5-0	4 times in 100 deals
9 cards	3-1	50 times in 100 deals
	2-2	40 times in 100 deals
	4-0	10 times in 100 deals
10 cards	2-1	78 times in 100 deals
	3-0	22 times in 100 deals
11 cards	1-1	52 times in 100 deals
	2-0	48 times in 100 deals

DIVISIONS OF OUTSTANDING HONORS

If opponents hold 2 honors: They will be divided 52 times in 100 deals; both will be in one hand 48 times in 100 deals

If opponents hold 1 honor:	Guarded Once	Guarded Twice
If they have: 3 cards it will be	52%	22%
4 cards it will be	40%	38%
5 cards it will be	28%	40%
6 cards it will be	18%	54%

HAND PATTERNS
(Distribution of four suits in one hand)

BALANCED PATTERNS	APPROXIMATE FREQUENCY	UNBALANCED PATTERNS	APPROXIMATE FREQUENCY
4-4-3-2	22%	4-4-4-1	3%
4-3-3-3	10%	5-4-3-1	13%
5-3-3-2	16%	5-5-2-1	3%
5-4-2-2	11%	6-4-2-1	5%
6-3-2-2	6%	6-3-3-1	3%
7-2-2-2	0.50%	5-5-3-0	0.90%
5-4-4-0	1.20%	6-5-1-1	0.70%
6-4-3-0	1.30%	7-3-2-1	1.80%

DUPLICATE METHODS

49

A full section is devoted to play in Culbertson's OFFICIAL BOOK and in the GOLD BOOK

DECLARER'S PLAY OF SUITS

To develop as many trick-winning cards as possible from the combined suit holdings of your hand and dummy, the mathematically correct methods are:

STRAIGHT LEADS

With solid honor holdings (three cards or more in sequence) usually lead out the honors and let the opponents take their higher honors, if any.

For example, with Ace, King and Queen; or King, Queen and Jack; or Queen, Jack and ten; lead or play an honor.

With long suits containing only low cards, lead out the low cards one by one until all the opponents' cards in the suit have been played.

With other suit holdings, play for a drop, or finesse.

PLAYS FOR A DROP

With **nine** or more cards in the combined hands, including Ace and King, lead out the Ace and King. (With nine cards, when the opponents have the Queen, the play for a drop is mathematically *slightly* better than a finesse, lacking contrary information from the bidding).

With **eleven** cards in the combined hands, including the Ace, lead the Ace. But with ten cards or less including A-Q, finesse as described below.

HOW TO FINESSE

With the following holdings, usually finesse. Extra low cards in either hand seldom affect the correct play.

YOU AND DUMMY HOLD:		WHAT TO DO
IN ONE HAND	IN OTHER HAND	(If Intervening Opponent Plays Low)
A-Q	x-x	*Lead toward A-Q. Play Q.*
A-Q-10	x-x-x	*Lead toward A-Q-10. Play 10. After that, play same as A-Q.*
A-Q-9	x-x-x	*Lead toward A-Q-9 and play 9. After that, play same as A-Q.*
A-K-J	x-x-x	*Cash the Ace. Later, lead toward K-J. Play J.*
A-K-10	x-x-x	*Lead toward A-K-10. Play 10.*

50

YOU AND DUMMY HOLD:		WHAT TO DO
A-J-10	x-x-x	*Lead toward A-J-10. Play 10. Next lead toward A-J. Play J.*
A-J-9	x-x-x	*Lead toward A-J-9. Play 9. Next lead toward A-J. Play J.*
A-x-x	Q-x-x or Q-J-x-x	*Cash Ace, then lead toward Q.*
A-x-x (Or A-x and Q-J)	Q-J-10	*Lead Q. Play low from A-x.*
A-K-Q-10	x-x	*Play Ace, then lead toward K-Q-10 and play 10. (But with seven or more cards of suit play for a drop.)*
K-x	x-x	*Lead toward K-x. Play the K.*
K-x-x	J-10-9	*Lead J. Play low from K-x-x.*
K-Q-10	x-x-x	*Lead toward K-Q-10. Play K. Next lead toward Q-10. If the K won the first trick, play Q. If the K lost the first trick, play 10.*
K-J-x	x-x-x	*Lead to K-J-x and play J. If it loses to Q, see play of K-x above.* With a doubleton in either hand, play *either* K or J on first round.
K-10-x	Q-x-x	*Lead toward Q. Play Q. Next lead toward K-10. Play 10.*
K-10-x or Q-10-x	x-x-x	*Lead toward high cards. Play 10. Next lead toward K-x (or Q-x) and play K (or Q).*
K-x-x	Q-x-x	*Lead toward either honor. Play the honor. If it wins, next lead toward other honor but play low.*
Q-J-x	x-x-x	*Lead toward Q-J-x. Play J. Next lead toward Q-x. Play Q.*
Q-x-x	J-9-x	*Lead toward Q-x-x. Play Q. Next lead toward J-9. Play 9.*

51

Even before playing to the first trick, stop to plan your play as follows:

1. **Always keep in mind** the contract, the number of tricks you have to win, and the maximum number of tricks you can afford to lose. From the previous bidding, and from the conventional meaning (pages 60–61) of the card led, try to get an idea of the nature of the defenders' hands.

2. **At a suit contract only:** If dummy has a short suit, in which you have cards which would otherwise be lost, try to void dummy in that suit and ruff your losers before playing out so many trumps that dummy will have none left to ruff with.

When there is no longer any need for dummy to ruff, usually lead the trump suit until the opponents have no more trumps in their hands.

3. **At notrump contracts particularly:** If the opponents' long suit is led against you, consider a hold-up play:

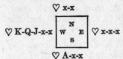

When West leads this suit, South purposely loses the first two leads and wins the third with his Ace. South may later lose the lead, but if he loses it to East, who now has no more hearts, West's two remaining hearts may never win tricks.

4. **Any suit,** including the trump suit at trump contracts, which is to be developed will be developed by straight leads, a play for a drop, or a finesse, all of which are described on pages 50–51.

5. **Count the entries you will need.** The play of most suits requires that one hand or the other specifically lead (pages 50–51). For each time it must lead, that hand must have an *entry-card*—that is, a card which will win a trick. Plan to conserve or to create as many entries as you need to develop the various suit holdings in your hand.

When South has taken his three high diamonds, North will have an entry in the ◊ 7, which will win over the ◊ 3. Note that if *South* wanted an extra entry, North would play ◊ 5, 6, 7 on ◊ A, K, Q and then South's ◊ 3 would win over the ◊ 2.

The ultimate in skill is card-reading. See Culbertson's OFFICIAL BOOK

6. Stoppers: A card or combination of cards which will win a trick in the opponents' strong suit is a stopper. Usually, the opponents themselves will lead this suit; you do not have to lead it. In general, avoid leading suits in which the opponents are stronger than you are (that is, in which they may ultimately win more tricks than you will). First try to develop suits in which you will win more tricks than your opponents will win.

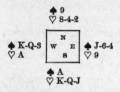

There are no trumps. South could win a trick immediately by taking his ♠ Ace. But then West would get the lead with the ♡ Ace, and his ♠ K-Q would win two more tricks. If instead South first leads a heart, West wins the first trick, but must then lead a spade. The ♠ Ace stops the suit and South wins *three* tricks.

7. Time valuation. In any suit you plan to develop, count the number of times the opponents must or may obtain the lead with high cards they hold in that suit. Then count the number of tricks they can establish and win with that number of leads. It may be that they can establish and win enough tricks to defeat your contract.

At notrump particularly, the suit in the partnership hands which promises to win the greatest number of tricks when developed is *usually* the suit to attack first; but time valuation may reveal that some shorter or less promising suit can more safely develop enough tricks to give you your contract.

8. At game contracts in a trump suit, it is usually easiest to count the number of tricks you must or may lose, and to base your plan on losing no more tricks than necessary. At game contracts in notrump, it is usually easiest to count the tricks you can win, and to base your plan on means of winning nine tricks, or as many more as you may need for your contract.

9. Always consider the possibility of a safety play (page 54). If you can surely make your contract, do not risk the contract to win extra tricks.

SAFETY PLAYS

See also
Finesses on
pages 50-51

When you can afford to lose *one trick* in the suit, but not *two*, play these holdings as follows:

IN ONE HAND	IN OTHER HAND	WHAT TO DO
A-K-8-x-x (or A-K-8-x & 10-x-x-x)	10-x-x	*Play Ace. If either opponent plays Q, J or 9, next lead low toward 10-x.*
A-Q-10-x-x (9 cards in combined hands, however distributed)	x-x-x-x	*Lead toward A-Q-10. If Jack shows up, play Queen; otherwise play Ace. Next lead toward Q-10.*
A-10-x-x-x (or A-9 and K-10)	K-9-x-x	*Lead low from either hand. Unless opponent shows out, play 9 (or 10) from other hand.*
K-J-x-x (or K-J-x-x-x and A-9-x, etc.)	A-9-x-x	*Take King. Then lead low toward A-9. Play 9 (unless opponent shows out.)*

With the following holdings, the play described is correct in all cases.

A-Q-x-x	x-x-x-x	*Play Ace. Then lead toward Q-x-x.*
A-9-x-x	Q-10-x-x	*Lead low toward A-9. Finesse 9. If it loses to Jack, next lead Queen and finesse.*
A-10-x-x-x (or the equivalent)	K-x-x-x	*Play King. Then lead toward A-10 and finesse 10.*
A-K-9-x-x (or the equivalent)	Q-x-x-x	*First, play Queen. Proper play will then be apparent.*
A-Q-9-x-x	J-x-x-x	*Lead Jack. Finesse (unless covered).*
A-Q-8-x-x	J-x-x-x	*Lead Jack. Finesse (unless covered).*
A-K-9-x-x (or the equivalent)	Q-10-x-x	*Take Ace (or King). Further proper play will then be apparent.*

Lacking entries, play as instructed on pages 50-51.

HOW TO CHOOSE YOUR LEAD

Against Trump Contracts

For the conventional card to lead from any suit see pages 60-61

The opening lead, being "blind," often loses a trick. *The most desirable lead is usually one that is safe.*

Best leads: An A-K-Q, or a long suit headed by A-K *(lead the King)*. You will win the first trick and can see dummy to guide your choice of a second lead, yet you still retain one or more *stoppers* in the suit. With A-K-x or even A-K-x-x, the lead is not so good, as it may sacrifice a valuable stopper *(see example on page 53)*. Any solid sequence (K-Q-J, Q-J-10, etc.) or a suit bid by partner (in which he probably has the high cards) is also a preferred lead.

Worst leads: A lead from a suit headed by honors *not in sequence* (such as A-Q) usually sacrifices a trick. *Avoid such suits* except when the bidding indicates that declarer's side has two long, solid suits which will give him his contract when run. *In such cases you must cash all winning cards immediately.*

Waiting leads: The lead of a worthless suit *cannot directly lose a trick.* The only damage it can do is to lose *time*—that is, waste a lead in which the defenders might establish or cash winning cards. Lacking a safe honor lead, usually lead a worthless short suit—including a 2- or 3-card holding in trumps.

Avoid, in most cases, any suit bid by the opponents, even though in that suit you have A-K or K-Q-J.

THE SLAM-LEAD CONVENTION

Any double of a slam contract—trump or notrump —warns the doubler's partner *not* to make his normal lead, such as the suit he or his partner has bid.

Your partner may double a trump slam when he is void in some suit and can ruff the opening lead. Holding a particularly long suit, even though it has been bid by the opponents, consider this possibility.

Or, your partner may have A-Q in a suit dummy has bid. Ordinarily, you would expect dummy to have the principal strength in this suit. If partner doubles a slam, consider opening such a suit.

BEST OPENING LEADS
Against Trump Contracts
CULBERTSON STANDARD TABLE
IN ORDER OF PREFERENCE

1. A-K-Q, A-K-J, A-K-x-x-x *with or without others.*

2. A trump *when Declarer has bid strongly in two suits, of which Dummy has supported only one.*

3. A or A-K *alone, with sure entry to Partner's hand and at least one ruffer.*

4. K-Q-J (-x-x-x)

5. A-x, K *or singleton[1] of Partner's suit.*

6. Singleton *with trump entry and at least one ruffer.*

7. Q-J-10 *or more, with no probable entry.*

8. Partner's suit, *with 4 or less. (See page 61).*

9. Q-J-10 *or more, with or without an entry.*

10. J-10-9-x *with or without others.*

11. A-K-x-x or A-K-x[2]

12. K-Q-10 *with or without others.*

13. Singleton *with 3 or more ruffers.*

14. Doubleton *containing no honor.*

15. A-x *with trump entry or when Partner has bid strongly.*

16. A or A-K *alone.*

17. 10-9-8-x

18. J-10-8-x

19. Trump x-x-x, x-x, A-x-x, K-x-x—*not a singleton.*

20. *Any suit which your partner has supported.*[3]

21. J-10, J-10-x, or Q-J *alone.*

22. A-x-x—*underlead A-x-x, A-x-x-x when bidding indicates that Dummy has a strong hand with balanced distribution.*

23. 10-9-7-x

24. x-x-x

For leads at Notrump Contracts see the next pages

25. x-x-x-x	32. J-x-x-x-(x)
26. Q-J-9-x̱	33. Q̱-J-x (x-x)
27. K̄-Q-x-x-x	34. A-x-x-x-x *or more*
28. J̄-10-x-x	35. K̄-x-x
29. K̄-x-x-x-(x)	36. Q-10-x̱
30. Q-x-x-x̱-(x)	37. 10̱-x-x
31. 10-x-x-x̱-(x)	

[1] A singleton of Partner's suit should not be led except when the object is to get a ruff

[2] A-K-x is often not so good as other leads ranked below it in this classification

[3] A suit headed by A-Q or A-J should usually not be opened, unless partner has supported it very strongly

LEADS TO BE AVOIDED

A-Q or A-Q-J	K-J-x or K-J-10-x
Singleton trump	A-J-x or A-J-10
Q-x-x or J-x-x	K-Q-x-x or K-Q-x-x
Q-x or J-x	K-x
A-x *except as in case 17*	K *alone*
A suit bid by the opponents	

LEADS AGAINST SLAM BIDS

Either six- or seven bids. Exceptions are marked (*).
See also "The Slam-Lead Convention," page 55.

	SUIT SLAM	NOTRUMP
Singleton.............	Good*	Very bad
Sequence of 3 honors...	Good	Good
Partner's suit.........	Good	Good
Ace...................	Fair**	Very bad**
Doubleton.............	Fair	Fair
Sequence of 2 honors...	Fair*	Bad
Trump 10-x-x *or* x-x-x..	Good	
Trump J-x, 10-x, x-x *or* x	Bad	
Q-x-x-x-x-x *or lower*....	Good	Fair
K-x-x-x *or* Q-x-x-x.....	Fair*	Very bad
x-x-x *or* x-x-x-x	Fair	Fair

*Very bad against Grand Slams   **Very good against Grand Slams.

LEADS AT

For the play of declarer at notrump see pages 52-53

OPENING LEADS AT NOTRUMP

To defeat a notrump contract, it is almost always necessary to establish a long suit. Remember the following four general principles in notrump leads.

1. In general try to open the longest and strongest suit in the combined hands.

Unless partner has bid, your own longest suit should usually be opened.

But if your longest suit has been bid by an opponent, do not open it unless it is long and solid (such as Q-J-10-9-x, K-Q-J-8-x, etc.).

2. If partner has bid a suit usually open that suit *unless*

(a) You have a singleton in partner's suit and a good suit of your own to lead; or

(b) You have a long solid suit and enough reëntries to defeat the opponents' contract alone (for example, K-Q-J-x-x with an Ace or King outside).

Likewise, if *you* have bid a suit and *partner has raised it,* it is probably your best opening lead.

3. If partner *doubles* the opponents' notrump bid, observe these rules:

If *partner* has bid a suit, open partner's suit.

If *you* have bid a suit and partner has *not,* open *your* suit.

If neither you nor partner has bid a suit, open a suit which *dummy* has bid *but not rebid,* and which declarer *has not raised.*

Otherwise, open as though partner had not doubled.

4. With a very weak hand, open a worthless 3-card suit or even a worthless doubleton.

You would probably never get in to run a long suit even if you could establish it.

Sometimes, even with a strong 4-3-3-3 or 4-4-3-2 hand, and no leadable sequence, a worthless short suit is a good *waiting lead,* so that declarer will have to lead to you in your strong suits.

BEST NOTRUMP LEADS
In Order of Preference

For leads at trump contracts see pages 55-57

The <u>CARD</u> to lead is underlined

1. An established suit *(lead the Ace).*
2. <u>A</u>-K-J-x-x-x-x *or better.*
3. <u>A</u>-K-Q-10-x, A-<u>K</u>-Q-x, A-<u>K</u>-Q-x-x. *But from A-K-Q-x-x lead fourth best with no entry* if partner probably has one.*
4. A-<u>Q</u>-J-10-x-x, A-<u>Q</u>-J-x-x-x-x. *But with a sure entry,* lead Ace.*
5. <u>K</u>-Q-J-x-(x-x)
6. <u>A</u>-K-x-x-x-x-x, K-Q-x-x-x-x-x, or <u>Q</u>-J-x-x-x-x-x *(7-card suit).*
7. <u>Q</u>-J-10-x-x *(or more).*
8. <u>A</u>-K-x-x-x, A-Q-x-x-x, A-J-x-x-x, K-Q-x-x-x *(5-card or 6-card suits).*
9. <u>Q</u>-J-10-x, <u>K</u>-Q-10-x, Q-J-9-x-x *or more.*
10. Any six-card suit *with an entry.**
11. Q-x-x-<u>x</u>-x, J-10-x-<u>x</u>-x *or better, with an entry.**
12. <u>J</u>-10-9-x, Q-10-x-<u>x</u>, x-x-x-<u>x</u>-x, *or better, with an entry.**
13. x-x-x-<u>x</u> *(from strong hands only).*
14. <u>x</u>-x-x, <u>10</u>-x-x, <u>J</u>-10-x.
15. <u>x</u>-x, <u>J</u>-10, <u>10</u>-x *(not Q-x or higher).*
16. <u>Q</u>-J-x, <u>K</u>-Q-x, A-<u>K</u>-x *(usually avoid).*

AVOID THE FOLLOWING LEADS
In the ordered named
(Except as gambling *desperation leads*).

1. Doubleton honor leads.
2. Three-card suits headed by one high honor, or two honors not in sequence.
3. Four-card suits headed by only the Ace, King or Queen, without Jack or 10.
4. Weak five-card suits in entryless hands.

LEADS AT NOTRUMP ✓

* An Ace, a King, and often a Q-J-x is a reasonably certain entry.

59

THE CARD TO LEAD

The following table assumes that you have already selected a *suit* to lead (pages 55–59) and indicates only the proper conventional *card* to lead.

CULBERTSON STANDARD TABLE OF
Conventional Leads

HOLDING IN SUIT	LEAD AT SUIT BIDS	LEAD AT NOTRUMP
A-K-Q-J *alone or with others*	K, *then* J	A*, *then* J
A-K-Q *with 3 or more others*	K, *then* Q	A, *then* K
A-K-Q-x-x *without a reëntry*	K, *then* Q	*Fourth best*
A-K-Q-x-x *or* A-K-Q-x	K, *then* Q	K, *then* Q
A-K-J-x-x-x-x *or more*	K, *then* A	A, *then* K
A-K-10-x-x-x-x *or more*	K, *then* A	A, *then* K
A-K-J-10-x-x *with a reëntry*	K	A
A-K-J-10 *alone or with others*	K	K
A-Q-J-x-x-x-x *or* A-Q-J-10-x-x *with a reëntry*	A	A
A-K-J, A-K-10, A-K *in 4-, 5-, or 6-card suit*	K, *then* A	*Fourth best*
A-Q-J-x *or longer*	A	Q
A-Q-10-9 *or longer*	A	10
A-J-10-x *or longer*	A	J
A-10-9-x *or longer*	A	10
A-x-x-x *or longer*	A	*Fourth best*
A-K-x	K, *then* A	K, *then* A
A-K *alone*	A, *then* K	*Avoid*
K-Q-J *alone or with others*	K, *then* J	K, *then* Q
K-Q-10 *alone or with others*	K	K
K-Q-x-x-x-x-x (7 *cards*) *or more*	K	K
K-Q-x-x-(x-x)	K	*Fourth best*
K-Q-x	K	K
K-Q *alone*	K	*Avoid*
K-J-10-x *or longer*	J	J

* The lead of the Ace of an unbid suit against a notrump contract is *conventional*, requesting that partner follow suit with his highest card, even the King or Queen, unless dummy reveals that the sacrifice of such a card would eventually lose a trick. The lead of a King against notrump may be used to call conventionally for partner's second highest card, but this convention is of doubtful value.

THE CARD TO LEAD (Continued)

See also signals in following suit and discarding— page 64

HOLDING IN SUIT	LEAD AT SUIT BIDS	LEAD AT NOTRUMP
K-10-9-x or longer	10	10
Q-J-10 *alone or with others*	Q	Q
Q-J-9 *alone or with others*	Q	Q
Q-J-x-x-x-x (*7 cards*)	Q	Q
Q-J-x-x-(x-x)	Q	*Fourth best*
Q-J-x	Q	Q
Q-J *alone*	Q	Q
Q-10-9-x or longer	10	10
J-10-9 *alone or with others*	J	J
J-10-8 *alone or with others*	J	J
J-10-x	J	J
J-10 *alone*	J	J
J-10-x-x or more	J	*Fourth best*
10-9-8 *alone or with others*	10	10
10-9-7 *alone or with others*	10	10
10-9-x-x or more	10	*Fourth best*
10-9 *alone or* 10-9-x *alone*	10	10
Any 4-card or longer suit not listed above	*Fourth best*	*Fourth best*

LEADS IN PARTNER'S BID SUIT

A-x, K-x, Q-x, J-x, 10-x, *or any other Doubleton*	*High card*	High card
J-10-x, 10-x-x or x-x-x	*Highest*	Highest
A-J-x, A-x-x, K-J-x, K-x-x, Q-10-x, Q-x-x, J-x-x	*Highest*	Lowest
Q-J-x-(x)	Q	Q
A-x-x-x *or better*	A	*Fourth best*
K-Q-x-(x)	K	K
Any other 4 or more cards	*Fourth best*	*Fourth best*

LEADS IN *UNBID* SHORT SUITS
At Trump or Notrump Contracts
The Card to Lead is Underlined

x-<u>x</u>	Q-x-<u>x</u>	K-x-<u>x</u>	K-<u>10</u>-9	A-<u>10</u>-9
x-x-<u>x</u>	Q-10-<u>x</u>	K-J-<u>x</u>	A-x-<u>x</u>	A-J-<u>x</u>
J-x-<u>x</u>	Q-10-<u>9</u>	K-10-<u>x</u>	A-<u>10</u>-x	A-J-10

Avoid leads from unbid short suits headed by an honor, except as *desperation* or *deceptive* leads.

DEFENDERS' PLAY

Conventional Follow-Suit Plays

On partner's low-card lead, usually play your highest card or *the lowest equivalent of your highest card.*
With Q-10-6, dummy holding J-3-2, if dummy plays low, play the 10, not the Queen.   With Q-10-9, play the 9, not the 10.   With K-Q-x, play the *Queen*, etc.

Remember. you *lead* the *highest* of equals, but you *play* the *lowest* of equals.

"Finesses Against Dummy"

When dummy has an honor, and you have a *higher* honor, in the suit led, usually *save your higher honor* to cover dummy's honor when it is played.   In this table, assume dummy's lowest card to be played:

Dummy Holds	You Hold	Partner Led	Play
K-x-x-(x)	A-J-x A-10-x A-9-x A-J-10	x	J 10 9 10
Q-x-x-(x)	A-J-x A-J-10 K-10-x K-9-x	x	J 10 10 9
J-x-x	Q-9-x K-10-x K-9-x	x	9 10 9
A-J-x	K-10-x Q-9-x	x	10 9

The Rule of Eleven

When you can assume your partner's lead to be his fourth-best, you may apply the Rule of Eleven:

Subtract the denomination (number of pips) of the card led from 11.

The result is the number of cards higher than the card led, held by other three players.

Then, since you know how many higher cards you hold, and can see the dummy, you can easily determine the declarer's holding.

When you can count (or infer) more higher cards in the other three hands than there could be under the Rule of Eleven, the lead is probably a short-suit lead.

HOW TO SIGNAL IN PLAY

For a fuller understanding of defenders' objective see GOLD BOOK by Ely Culbertson

In discarding, a player should be careful not to sacrifice a necessary *guard* to an honor. (An Ace requires no guard, but if unguarded may cause the suit to be blocked). Discards and follow-suit plays can also signal valuable information to partner, as follows:

Encouraging Signals. Play (or discard) an *unnecessarily high card, not your lowest*. This (called the *come-on*) tells partner to lead, or continue leading, the suit. When possible, next play (or discard) a *lower* card—this is a *high-low*, or *echo*, and confirms your previous encouraging card. With a doubleton, if you want to ruff a third round, play high-low.

Discouraging Signals. The play (or discard) of your *lowest* card in a suit warns partner *not* to lead it. Do not, however, sacrifice a possible trick-winner or stopper solely to make an encouraging play or a high-low signal. Sometimes, low discards in *other* suits may steer partner to a suit in which you cannot conveniently give a come-on signal.

Distributional Echoes. To play high-low *in the trump suit* tells partner *you still have a trump left*, and (usually) that you want to ruff a lead in some other suit. Do not high-low in trumps without at least three trumps.

In the opponents' strong suit, with only worthless cards of the suit in your hand, in following suit first play your *lowest* if you have *exactly three cards;* play high-low with *two* cards or *four* cards in the suit.

The Suit-Preference Signal.* Expert players may use this more subtle signal: When leading a card for partner to ruff; or when following suit or discarding, *provided the card played cannot logically be one of the signals described above;*

The play of a *very high* card tells partner next to lead the *higher-ranking available suit* (other than trumps);

The play of a *low* card calls for the *lower-ranking* of those suits.

* Developed by Hy Lavinthal of Trenton, New Jersey

For the
conventional
meaning of the
card LED see
pages 60-61

WHEN TO COVER AN HONOR

Usually, when an honor is led, and you hold a higher honor in the same suit, you should cover with your honor if you believe partner *may* hold a combination such as J-x, 10-x-x, 9-x-x-x, Q-9-x, etc.

This table gives the play which is *usually* correct:

DUMMY HOLDS	YOU HOLD	CARD LED	PLAY
Q-J-10-(x-x)	K-x-x-(x)	Queen	Low, all leads
Q-J-9-x-x	K-x-x	Queen, then Jack	Low, both leads
Q-J-9-x	K-x-x or K-10-x	Queen, then Jack	Low, first lead, cover second
Q-x-(x-x)	K-x-(x-x)	Queen	cover*
J-10-x-x-x	K-x-x or Q-x-x	Jack, then 10	Low, both leads
J-10-x-x	A-Q-9	Jack	cover
J-10-x	K-x-x or Q-x-x	Jack, then 10	Low, first lead, cover second
J-x-(x-x) or 10-x-(x-x)	K-x-x or Q-x-x	Jack or ten	cover*
10-x-x-(x) or 10-9-x-(x)	J-x-x-(x)	10	low
J-x-x	K-Q-x	Jack	cover
A-x-x-(x)	K-x-x-(x)	Queen or Jack	low
A-x-x-(x)	Q-x-x-(x)	Jack	low
A-x-x-(x)	K-9-x	Queen or Jack	Cover Queen Low on Jack
A-x-x	K-10-x	Queen or Jack	Cover Queen Low on Jack
A-x-x or K-x-x	Q-x-(x) or J-x-(x)	10	low
Q-x-x	J-x-x	10	low

* When partner may have a singleton in the suit, do not cover.

UNUSUAL HANDS

NORTH	EAST	SOUTH
S - AKQJ3	S - 64	S - 1098752
H - AQ	H - KJ10862	H -
D - AKQ3	D - J542	D - 109876
C - KQ	C - 9	C - J10

WEST
S -
H - 97543
D -
C - A8765432

EW CAN MAKE 6 HEARTS

NS CANNOT MAKE 6 IN ANYTHING

NORTH	EAST	SOUTH
C - AKQJ653	C -	C - 42
S - 75	S - 10643	S - J982
D - A93	D - 1087642	D - 5
H - 3	H - 754	H - AKQ10 62

WEST
C - 10987
S - AKQJ
D - KQJ
H - J98

W	N	E	S
INT	2C	P	2H
P	3C	P	3H
P	4C	P	P
DOUB	P	P	4H
DOUB	5C	P	P
DOUB	P	P	P